KU-548-440

N 0024442 2

Developments in Drama Teaching

The Changing Classroom

General Editor: John Eggleston

Developments in Art Teaching
Terence Wooff

Developments in Design Education
John Eggleston

Developments in Drama Teaching
Lynn McGregor

Developments in Early Childhood Education
Janet Lancaster and Joan Gaunt

Developments in English Teaching
Michael Saunders

Developments in Geography Teaching
Philip Boden

Developments in History Teaching
Ian Steele

Developments in Mathematics Teaching
F. R. Watson

Developments in Modern Language Teaching
Colin Wringe

Developments in Social Studies Teaching
Denis Gleeson and Geoff Whitty

Developments
in
Drama Teaching

Lynn McGregor

Open Books
London

First published in 1976 by Open Books Publishing Ltd,
87–89 Shaftesbury Avenue, LONDON W1V 7AD

Hardback: ISBN 0 7291 0007 3

Paperback: ISBN 0 7291 0002 2

Text set in 11/12 pt Photon Imprint, printed by photolithography, and bound in Great Britain at The Pitman Press, Bath

Contents

Acknowledgement

I would like to thank the teachers for allowing me access to their work.

Editor's introduction

The theme of this series of books is the changing classroom. Everyone knows that schools change – that despite all the influences of tradition things aren't the same as they used to be. Yet during the past decade the change has been on such an unprecedented scale that in many ways schools have become surprising places not only to those who work with them – like parents and employers – but even to those who work in them, like teachers and students.

There are many reasons for these changes. Some are organisational, like the move to comprehensive secondary schooling, the raising of the school leaving age, new pre-school classes, and 'destreaming', where children of all abilities work together. But even more spring from the way the teacher works in the classroom – from the increasing emphasis on individual methods, on creativity rather than remembering, on new patterns of assessment and examination, and on the use of a wide variety of project methods.

Such changes have certainly transformed the life of many classrooms and made school a different place for teachers and their students. This series is about life in those classrooms, for it is here that we can not only see change but understand it and get to grips with its effects on young people and on the society in which they will live.

In this volume Lynn McGregor writes about new developments in the teaching of drama. What is this new subject that increasingly features in the curriculum of many schools? In what way does it offer experiences beyond those of the traditional school play? How may the expressive opportunities it can give help the student's all round development? How does it link with the creative use of language encouraged by English teachers? Lynn McGregor, an experienced teacher of drama and leader of the Schools Council Drama Project, is well placed to answer these questions, and offers an exciting account of the possibilities of drama in the curriculum with a wealth of illustration of current work in the schools.

John Eggleston

Introduction

Educational drama as it is now taught is a relatively new subject. Some of the main exponents are active and influential today. Although drama is becoming more popular in many schools, there is no general consensus or agreement on precisely what the subject entails. This is because it is firstly a way of teaching rather than a subject incorporating a set body of knowledge. In addition, drama encompasses a number of educational concepts and activities. Because of this there is often disagreement among teachers about what is best practice.

This book begins by giving a general outline of some of the main kinds of drama found in schools. The central justifications for the subject are mentioned. A short description of the state of the subject in schools then follows. This is concerned with the ways in which drama is organised in school, with how drama is timetabled and with the kinds of facilities allocated; it attempts to give some indication of the present status of the subject, and to explain some of the difficulties drama teachers encounter in schools. Some consideration is given to how drama compares with the teaching of other subjects. By doing this I hope to put the subject in the context of the school before discussing some of the central concepts and activities inherent in the subject.

The first part of the book is an attempt to discuss general areas of agreement on what drama is about and how it is practised. It is based on a summary of existing written work and deals with such concepts as acting, play, imagination and creativity, social, verbal and physical education, creative problem solving, the use of drama as an art form, and the relevance of performance in drama. Emphasis is placed on those general areas of theory and practice in which there is agreement.

However, as already mentioned, within the subject there are broad areas of controversy. These include the debate over whether the educational value of drama is experiential and exploratory, or whether it is valid to work towards performance. Some feel that child drama has nothing to do with 'showing' or theatre whereas others feel that it should lead to theatre. Finally, the importance of discussion is mentioned, as some teachers feel that discussion should not be a part of dramatic activity while for others it serves as a focal point for the lesson.

This first part of the book should be a background for the case studies, which represent different ways in which drama is taught. Each case study takes the type of school and pupils into account. This section of the book consists of descriptions of sessions or courses with comments by the teachers. As well as descriptions of differences in practice, some mention is made of the reasons drama teachers have for working in certain ways. It is hoped that the five case studies will indicate some of the activities possible in drama, and show where polarities of concepts and practices occur.

The final part begins with an account of those aspects of the subject that are being currently discussed in drama circles and points to some of the issues thought important and questions that are currently being asked. These range from the need for a conceptual framework justifying the distinctive role educational drama can play in schools today, to the need for teachers to be able to evaluate their work. Changing trends of lesson structures are mentioned – for example, some teachers are moving away from an emphasis on individual development to that of the whole class.

A discussion of these issues helps to indicate the theoretical direction in which the subject is going. However, it is equally important to return to the context of the school and to discuss how possible curriculum changes might affect drama. Two contrasting directions are mentioned: the growing importance of formal examinations on the one hand and, on the other, the increasing propensity of some teachers to follow an integrated child centred syllabus in which drama is one activity. Some account is also taken of general trends in curricula changes and how drama might be affected, for example the effects of block timetabling.

The final chapter is concerned with possible lines of enquiry in addition to those already mentioned. It is suggested that attention be given to aspects which include the general educational context of drama, and that some research be done about stages of child development relevant to the subject. It is also suggested that the question of educational drama versus theatre be reopened both in terms of the theoretical and practical links between them as well as the cultural significance of performances in schools. For instance the continuation and importance of the school play cannot be ignored because some drama teachers disapprove of it.

The contents of the book are based on a mixture of consideration of written work, discussion held with drama specialists, observation of drama sessions and, finally, my own teaching experience.

PART I

The present state of drama: theory and controversy

1 Drama in schools

Kinds of drama found in schools: some justifications for the subject

Everybody, especially children, plays games of make-believe. People imagine what it is like to be certain people or to be in various situations. Usually this takes place in the mind. In drama it is acted out. In drama in schools, the activity is thought to have educational value. Some teachers claim that by doing drama pupils can gain a deeper understanding of people and of situations. Trying to be in someone else's shoes and to imagine how characters would react in certain situations gives a physical, visual and immediate experience which is different from that of reading, writing or discussing the same things. Through drama it is possible to examine things on a social and interpersonal level. Drama can therefore be a means of understanding various aspects of behaviour, including interpersonal relations, feelings and the exploration of social issues such as conflict situations. Children can interpret their feelings and understanding of social situations and express them through dramatic form.

Because 'educational drama' involves working with other people, it allows groups of children to work together creatively. They are often given ideas to work on and expected to come up with some dramatic statement about these ideas. They are sometimes expected to communicate their work to others. The process of 'creative problem solving' is thought by some teachers to be more important than the actual results.

Two aspects of educational drama epitomise the main kinds of emphasis that occur within the field. The first, which I call 'learning through drama', emphasises the exploration of issues and people through drama. It is an exploration which involves both the teacher and the pupils and usually results in discussion of the issues involved. It can be used as a method to teach particular subjects such as history or social studies.

The second kind of drama envisages drama as an art form in its own right. It lays responsibility on the children to work on the stimuli given by the teacher. Usually the teacher plays a relatively passive role, except when she helps students with difficulties and with finding ways of saying what they want to say more effectively in dramatic terms. This kind of activity means that pupils have to produce ideas, decide among themselves to put them together and then create a scene with its own characters and situations which is meaningful to them and sometimes to others. The value lies in the creative process as well as in the experience of working constructively and responsibly with other people.

Both kinds of drama described occur in schools today. They are commonly used in the first three years in one or both forms, depending on the methods teachers adopt. Children are not usually examined for these kinds of drama unless they are linked to a specific course – usually a 'theatre arts' course. There are, however, a few examinations which are 'drama' rather than 'theatre' based. This book is mainly concerned with 'drama' based practice as it is more widely used in schools.

'Theatre arts' is usually taught in the context of traditional forms of drama and is closely connected with the professional theatre. In the upper school, usually the fourth and fifth forms, option groups are taught the subject. It usually involves a course which includes a short history of the theatre, the performance of a play based on improvisation, the study of set plays and finally a finished performance of a scripted play. This course often leads to an examination, either a C.S.E. or O level. An A level course is also in the process of being agreed. These courses are supposed to give children a wider appreciation of drama as an art form, a background knowledge of the theatre and some plays written for the theatre; and experience in the work involved in putting on plays, both in terms of stage management and acting for performance.

The form of drama most commonly seen in schools is seldom part of the general school curriculum. It involves usually a great many children in the school of all ages, the staff, some parents, and serves as a link between the school and the community. This is the school play. Many people across the school cooperate to produce a performance. The school play is therefore both culturally and socially significant. It could be used as an example to show those cynical about the value of drama that drama is an integral part of the general culture of the school and could be developed as a useful natural learning resource.

I have given a general description of some of the ways in which drama can be taught in schools. Within the main kinds of teaching, other activities could occur which may include things like acting exercises, movement, games, interaction exercises, mime and many other activities associated with drama. These are usually used to improve the state of drama rather than as ends in themselves.

Apart from the school play, which occurs in almost all schools regardless of whether they have drama on the timetable or not, drama as a subject is not universally accepted in all schools.

One of the problems is that people do not know what drama is about and many drama teachers are unable to articulate their case for the subject. Other teachers often confuse what happens in the drama room with the school play or with training for the theatre. These activities are generally regarded as not essential to the everyday curriculum of the school. Some drama teachers focus on the importance of children expressing their own ideas and have an informal relationship with the children. Because of this in more formal schools complaints have been made that the subject is subversive. Non-drama teachers complain that children come into their lessons either too lively or too tired. Traditional teachers who do not know much about the subject have been heard to say that it is merely an excuse for chaos. They feel that their claims are justified because the noise level when drama takes place is often high. Where there are no proper facilities this means that other lessons are disturbed.

Where there is support for the subject it is usually because of vague notions that drama helps the social, imaginative and creative development of the child. Because the process of 'acting' often involves speech and therefore language, and because a lot of drama is traditionally based on the reading of scripts, the majority of drama teachers were until recently placed in the English department in secondary schools. This sometimes meant that they were working with people who either did not understand the principles behind drama or were hostile towards it. Occasionally it means that drama is taught by all the members of an English department – often by people who have not been trained to teach drama. The situation is beginning to change and it might be useful to look at the present state of the field so that the subject can be seen in relation to other subjects and its place in various schools.

The state of the subject in schools

It is almost impossible to get accurate figures of where and how much drama is taught in schools. This is especially so in primary schools where drama is taught by non-specialists and very much on an ad hoc basis. From conversations with some teachers who do teach drama regularly in primary schools, and with members of the advisory services who see it in schools, a number of factors emerge which indicate that drama may not be fully used in primary schools. At present a Schools Council survey of primary schools is being conducted in an attempt to see what is happening.

DRAMA IN PRIMARY SCHOOLS

As far as it is possible to tell, most teachers in primary schools who teach drama see it as a part of general studies rather than as a specialist subject. Some see it as a way of extending, for instance, English or history or as a particular way of developing, for example, language. A great deal of drama in primary schools, however, is movement based. This is mainly because drama is generally done in the school hall which is shared by other teachers. Each class is usually able to use the hall once a week. Teachers therefore wish to make the maximum use of the space available and will tend to see it as best suited to various forms of physical expression.

DRAMA IN SECONDARY SCHOOLS

The most recent survey done on drama teaching in schools was in 1975 (Robinson 1975). Although Robinson's survey only deals with 259 schools, it could be argued that a study of these gives a reasonable indication of the state of the subject. His findings are similar to those found by an 'Arts and the Adolescent' project and are confirmed by various H.M.I.s who say that it accurately reflects the picture. According to the survey, more comprehensive schools have drama than other schools. It seems that very little drama takes place in either grammar, secondary modern, technical or independent schools.

The kind of teachers teaching drama The survey suggests that in schools where there are drama specialists it is unusual to have three or four specialists and almost unknown to have more than four. There are often two specialists but most common are schools which have one specialist, and about a quarter of the schools with drama on the timetable had no specialists. Most of the non-specialists teaching drama were English teachers and in schools where there were a number of drama teachers, there were less English teachers than usual. In the total number of schools studied, there were almost twice as many specialists as there were non-specialists. These figures included teachers who had had some drama training but who mainly taught other subjects.

Specialist drama teachers were mainly employed in lower, middle and working class comprehensives and secondary modern schools. Even there there were not many (i.e. 11 per cent) compared to subjects like English (43 per cent), art (25 per cent) and music (20·4 per cent). In schools where there were a greater number of specialists, the figures rose by one or two per cent.

Not all teachers employed to teach drama were trained to teach the subject. For example, a fifth of the teachers teaching drama had had no drama training. Perhaps there is a greater need for the subject than there exist specialists to teach it. Most teachers trained to teach drama came from colleges of education. Fifty-two per cent of the specialists took the subject there as a main course and over half of those who took drama as a subsidiary course took it in a college of education. There were very few graduates.

Fifteen years ago, almost all drama teachers worked within the English department. 56·6 per cent of the sample of schools still placed drama within the English department. 38 per cent had drama departments (usually comprehensive schools). A small number came under a faculty of creative arts (1·4 per cent) and 0·4 per cent of drama teaching was found in the art department.

It is often usual to see posts advertised for 'English and Drama Specialists' which indicates that English teachers are often expected to be able to teach drama.

The amount and allocation of drama in schools Forty per cent of specialist teachers were found to work alone. This generally meant that they taught many children throughout the school. Of these, only 16 out of 294 teachers taught drama for the whole week. Most specialists taught drama for less than twenty hours a week. Many drama teachers taught more English than drama. It is therefore not surprising that a lot of drama takes place within English lessons.

Where non-specialists taught drama, they normally did not teach more than five hours a week. Frequently drama was used by other subject teachers as a 'one off' lesson to extend their own work; e.g. a lesson on the United Nations could be followed by a simulated debate.

From these figures it follows that the full potential of drama is not used in schools.

In the majority of schools where drama was on the timetable (about 8 per cent), it was compulsory in the first two years. In the third year, however, some schools offered a choice between drama and alternative subjects and others had a certain amount of drama that was compulsory and some choice on top of that.

Drama was mainly optional in the fourth and fifth years, and had to compete with examination oriented subjects. In the same survey, the number of drama courses in the fourth year dropped by 47·6 per cent, showing that for most children drama stops when they are fourteen. In the fourth and fifth years an increasing number of teachers are offering the subject as an examination course. There are a number of C.S.E. Mode III drama courses and a small but growing number of teachers are teaching O level drama.

There appears to be very little drama in the sixth form. In the study, only 31 per cent of the schools offered any drama at this stage.

Most schools allow thirty to forty minutes of drama per week in the first three years. A few allow sixty to eighty minutes. I have observed a few schools in which drama is part of creative arts, in which subjects are blocked for three hours a week. Each subject rotates with other subjects once a term. Class numbers vary between twenty and thirty although some teachers are known to work with more than forty children.

Because courses in the fourth and fifth years are optional and often entail working for examinations, classes are smaller – between ten and twenty. They have between 120 and 160 minutes a week. In the sixth forms numbers often dwindle to about ten and the amount of time is often similar to that of the fourth and fifth forms.

Compared to most other subjects, the amount of time available for children to learn drama is limited. It is evident that the subject does not enjoy a high status. This is reflected in the type of facilities and resources given to drama teachers. In only 50 per cent of the schools studied were there either custom built studios or halls or spaces converted for the use of drama. Most of these were used for other things, for example, other lessons, assemblies or performances. In many cases drama teachers had to teach wherever there was a space – classrooms, cloakrooms, houserooms, halls or gymnasiums. Many teachers teaching in houserooms or halls were constantly interrupted by people getting ready for dinners or clearing up afterwards. Teachers were often expected to set up furniture for dinners or for other lessons. This meant that their amount of time for drama was curtailed. Although it is generally agreed that often the use of music, sound effects and lighting can give atmosphere and enhance concentration, not all the teachers studied had access to sound equipment and far fewer to lighting equipment. Drama could indeed be said to be a poor relation in the curriculum of most schools.

Conclusion

Thus we have a picture of a subject which is not fully established and which is thought by some to have no need of specialists. The subject has, however, expanded greatly since the forties when there could hardly have been more than a handful of drama teachers. In the last fifteen years courses in colleges of education have increased and there are now nearly eighty drama advisers in the country. The subject has been given 'scarcity' status by the government which indicates that there is more demand for drama teachers than there are specialists to go round. The recognition of the usefulness of drama is also shown by the large number of non-specialists teaching it. Although the subject is relatively new in Britain, drama teaching has been in existence here for longer than in most countries and has developed in sophistication since it began. Because of this educators from all over the world are visiting Britain to study this field.

In spite of this, teachers are still having a struggle to get the subject accepted in their schools. Many other members of staff are still cynical about drama and feel it to be a waste of time. As drama teachers are often unable to articulate their aims and objectives clearly, and as there are a variety of views about the purposes and practices of drama, the subject seems to lack any coherent rationale and people are therefore reluctant to give it the status of a discipline in its own right. However, if common assumptions and practices could be found in all the different practices, a case for the subject as a distinctive educational feature could be made.

At the beginning of this chapter, a brief outline was given of some of the justifications for drama. In the next chapter, I intend to go deeper into the central concepts and activities found in the subject which are taken for granted by many drama teachers and which form the basis of much drama teaching.

2 What is drama? Some central concepts and activities

A brief outline of 'educational drama'

The picture given here will be drawn from the writings of some of the main exponents of drama teaching. It is a general picture and attempts to find out what common assumptions underlie most drama teaching. I shall give a brief outline of the types of activity generally thought to come within the province of 'drama in education' and then describe some of the different approaches prescribed by drama teachers. This will be followed by an analysis of some of the educational aims found in common in most of these approaches. The purpose is to give a general picture of what kind of subject drama is rather than to discuss ideological differences. Neither is it an analysis of lesson content – this will be given later in the book.

Many people hearing the word 'drama', associate it with 'theatre'. In education this conjures up images of the performance of the school play, with pupils acting on a stage in front of an audience, usually from a script. It might also be thought of as a training for the theatre – through the learning of acting techniques, direction, stage management and general history of the theatre. In many schools this aspect of drama is taught as a C.S.E. subject, so it cannot be dismissed as unimportant. It is, however, only one facet of 'educational drama' and is totally disregarded by some drama teachers.

Many teachers feel that the main importance of drama comes from the intrinsic value of being involved in 'acting'. In other words, they believe that children learn something by playing different roles in imagined situations. This attitude could be said to derive from theories of acting which suggest that in order to portray characters realistically and in depth, it is important for the actor to act as if he were the character himself. The actor creates an image of the character by *improvising* situations which he feels his assumed character might experience. In this way he can accumulate enough details relevant to the character and situation to portray it with substance.

Improvisation is therefore thought to be an important aspect of acting and could be said to be the basis of drama teaching. However, it varies in type and emphasis, as will be seen in the next section. It usually involves action in both a physical and verbal sense (many drama teachers feel that both these aspects – movement and speech – are important for children).

VARIOUS APPROACHES TO DRAMA TEACHING

Much of the work drama teachers do consists of a mixture of approaches and activities. Described below are the main areas of difference:

1 Movement and mime
2 Teacher directed drama
3 Teacher directed drama using role play
4 Child centred group improvisations
5 The use of games
6 The use of drama as a service
7 Study of drama as training for the theatre

Some of these will be illustrated in more detail in Part II.

1 Movement and mime This involves some type of expressive use of the body. There are three main ways in which movement is used in classrooms. The first is where children are asked to imagine that they are in a certain physical environment and then to act in mime as though they are. Often the teacher directs their movements. 'One begins by thinking of innumerable classes of boys and girls lying on the floor . . . and doing exercises in relaxation and contraction. Then they begin to move, sometimes in a heavy and contracted manner, sometimes, by contrast, as snowflakes . . .' For instance, the teacher might ask pupils to imagine they are lying on a beach, that then it gets cold, they get up, stretch, put some clothes on and so on.

The second type of movement is formal mime which involves precise and traditional ways of creating illusions through formalised movements, simulating the opening of doors, the climbing of walls and so on. Pupils build up a repertoire of such movements which they are then asked to incorporate into scenes.

The third type of movement is one in which different parts of the body and space are explored and the main emphasis is on building up personal relationships through physical contact. For instance Veronica Sherborne (1973), at a conference 'on the exceptional child', said: 'awareness of others and awareness of body have been my main areas of exploration. . . . It is against another person and through another person, that the young child discovers who he is'. Examples of this type of movement could show pupils being supported by each other or the teacher, balancing their weight against each other to build up trust or pushing and pulling in such a way that no one is hurt.

This type of activity is usually done in pairs or small groups, in contrast to the next type, which is usually done with the class as a whole.

2 Teacher directed drama Peter Slade (1964) developed this form of acting for what he called 'imagination training', which involves total absorption in playing parts. An example of this type of drama could be in acting out the story of Theseus and the Minotaur. Every child would play Theseus and would act out the story according to the teacher's direction while narrating the story. This would often be done with music. This form of activity is based on the notion that by being asked to imagine situations entirely outside his experience, the child's perceptions of his own world are expanded.

3 Teacher directed drama using role play This is an approach which concentrates not so much on fantasy but on subject matter that is of social relevance to pupils. It is often done with a teacher taking part in the acting and also directing the sequence of events.

One of the early tasks of the teacher is to create experiences of intensity . . .

because these are the ones which will commit the class to further work as they give instant feedback. . . . It is at once simpler and more economical to achieve this for the whole class. . . . a crowd . . . suddenly hearing the voices or marching feet of troops will have their attention arrested even momentarily. (Heathcote 1971)

Sometimes small groups are asked to go away and work on situations related to some social theme that the teacher feeds them. The emphasis, however, remains on the activities of the whole class. Activity is directed through the teacher who takes on a role and acts as a focal point for the situation explored.

4 Child centred group improvisations Here the emphasis is on subject matter chosen by the children themselves, so that dramatic activity can begin at the particular stage of development of the group of children concerned. Children are often asked to suggest a situation (e.g. robbing a bank) and to go away and create a scene around it. Group work is thought to be important for social development. For example, Brian Way (1969) saw small groups 'as a collection of individual efforts stimulated and sustained by the existence of a group, often with exchange of ideas or prompted suggestions during the actual doing of any activity'. Children are expected to provide their own ideas and then shape them into a dramatic form that satisfactorily expresses the ideas they have been experimenting with.

5 The use of games Whereas small group improvisation could be said to involve children in creating their own scenes and rules of play, games have been used to improve interpersonal relationships in more structured situations. Children work within rules rather than create them. An example of a game could be that of 'statues' for younger children or a cumulative game where pupils are asked to reconstruct the details of a crime by accurately building on what has been said before.

6 The use of drama as a service In many secondary schools drama has been seen as part of English and has been used by teachers to illustrate points they have been trying to make about, for example, literature. For instance, John Hodgson has made use of improvisation in helping children to understand the *Romeo and Juliet* situation by acting out similar situations of family conflict in modern idiom.

This method can also be used in such subjects as history, religious instruction or any other subject which involves interpersonal relationships.

7 Training for theatre Here drama is seen as a specific art form related to traditional theatre. There is usually a set syllabus including a study of the history of the theatre, stage management and the producing of unscripted and scripted performances at the end of the course. Examinations are sometimes taken, e.g. C.S.E. theatre arts or O level drama.

Another way in which the professional theatre is brought nearer to schools is through 'Theatre in Education' teams which visit schools and give performances. Sometimes they give traditional performances of plays set for examinations; sometimes they are more community based, using audience participation.

In the last few pages I have given a short summary of the different kinds of drama advocated. It is interesting that some of their main exponents are still active and can be observed teaching. For instance, Peter Slade has a centre in Birmingham and Brian Way in London. Although Brian Way introduced the approach which concentrates on small group work, he has moved away from that position to one closer to theatre in education and has a large team of performers. Although I have isolated different activities and ways of working, Brian Way's change illustrates that not all drama teachers confine their activities to one way of working. This is possibly because implicit in most drama teaching are values and assumptions that cut across the differences.

COMMON ASSUMPTIONS FOUND IN EDUCATIONAL DRAMA

The assumptions below are based on what people think drama is about and what they think the subject ought to (rather than does) contain.

Imagination and creativity All the approaches mentioned involve participation of pupils through acting. Drama is therefore a subject that sees activity, i.e. 'doing', as important. It is based on the premise that everyone can act, and can learn from his experience of the activity. The capacity to act as if you are in a different situation or are playing another character presupposes imagination. Imagination, developed sufficiently, enables one to extend one's perceptions beyond what is immediately seen, to allow for more than one possible solution to occur, and to see situations and people in more than one way.

If pupils are asked to act as if they are in imaginary situations, they have to create the characters and situations explored. They need to be able to react immediately to the circumstances in which they are placed (e.g. what do you do if you are faced with eviction and the men have come to take your things away?). If children are asked to work in groups on a stimulus, they have to create shape out of their ideas. Without creativity, drama could not occur.

The concepts of imagination and creativity could be said to be essential ingredients in all drama. These are usually focussed on understanding human behaviour in terms of how people feel and behave in certain situations.

Play Dramatic activity is thought by many to be an extended form of play. Play is thought of as the natural way that children learn and drama is useful in developing play so that children can extend themselves creatively and constructively. What is to be taught is geared to the needs of the pupils at the particular time of teaching. This is emphasised by many exponents including Peter Slade, Brian Way, and Veronica Sherborne, who says (1973):

> One of my main jobs is to help students and teachers to play, and to teach through play. The material, or content, has to be adapted according to the needs of the different groups, and how 'awareness of others' is developed depends on the teacher's sensitivity in observing the group.

Many claims have been made about the value of play in drama. They include the developing of children's natural ability to explore their world and find meaning in it. Through play children learn to get on with others and to find out how they stand in relation to others. It enables them to explore fantasy in safe conditions and to come to terms with it. It is a way in which, through make believe, children can explore those things that interest them at that particular stage of development (for instance, ghosts) and perhaps come to terms with some deep seated fears and misunderstandings.

Connected with the importance of development through activity is the implicit assumption that uniqueness of response is valued. Through drama, children ought to be able to express and communicate their feelings and understandings in their own ways. But their response is not only 'personalised'; in drama, it is basically social.

The social aspect of drama There are very few occasions in drama when a pupil is expected to work by himself for a long period of time, rather than with a group, another person or with the class as a whole. A number of reasons are given for this. For instance, Veronica Sherborne (1973) suggests that it is important to 'activate . . . mutual help between children through exercises designed to promote "sharing and sensitivity"'. 'It is against another person, and through another person, that the young child discovers who he is.'

Brian Way (1969) to some extent agrees with her. 'Drama helps the indigenous qualities of the person making the effort, partly by increasing the sensitivity to the responsibilities involved in all facets of sharing with other people.' However, he sees group drama primarily as teaching children to take responsibility: 'Our primary objective is that of handing over some of the responsibility for the "what" and "who" as well as for the "how".'

Gavin Bolton (1971) believes that 'when drama is a group sharing of a dramatic situation it is more powerful than any other medium in education'. His conception of what pupils learn from group experience is wider than that of group experiences of sharing and caring. One of his aims is 'to help the student know how and when (and when not) to adapt to the world he lives in. This presupposes that drama helps the child determine for himself the sort of world he wishes to life in. In this sense it could be said to contain some of the subversive elements that some teachers accuse it of having'.

Creative problem solving through drama Connected with the idea that drama is a social activity, many of the approaches see drama as some form of problem solving. For example a group of children will be told to go away and create a scene about a family conflict where a teenager wants to leave home. Two types of problems need to be solved: that of the group working together and creating something and the actual problem set by the theme. This type of drama is well summed up by Dorothy Heathcote (1971), who says:

> ... It is the awareness of the class creating the play that we want to stimulate.... We create an opportunity for a collecting of attitudes to relate together in problem solving.... All the attitudes ... can provide the spectrum for solving the problem ... then ... there is opportunity for a widening sphere of attitudes and problems and therefore a greater number of relationships and associations ... to be brought into orbit and made available to the group.

When groups of children work together on problem solving in drama, they are working towards a dramatic form in which to express their solutions. This sometimes has meaning only to them and sometimes can be communicated to others; then it is the finished scene that is performed, and which serves as a communicating link between them and others.

Performance Dramatic activities are not always performed in front of an audience. When they are, they are sometimes a result of children wanting to communicate their work to others. Children are sometimes asked to improvise in front of others when teachers want to experiment with or highlight particular things, e.g. interview situations. Both these kinds of performance are usually done in the classroom in front of peers.

Most public performances are performances of scripted plays on a stage, costumed, with lighting and sound effects. These performances are more closely linked with the kind of drama seen in the traditional theatre.

Whenever performances occur, the main emphasis is on communication and on how the play is presented. This means that people have to coordinate their activities so that the scenes run smoothly and actors concentrate on being seen, heard and understood. Communication skills are often taught to facilitate performance.

ATTITUDES WITH REGARD TO CHILDREN, RELATIONSHIPS, AND TEACHING METHODS

Having given a brief outline of the subject based on existing written material, it might be useful to summarise the assumptions in such a way that they could be compared to those underlying the teaching of other subjects.

Except for drama as 'theatre', there is no stress on the importance of the *acquisition of knowledge*. As with progressive education in general, concepts of child development and play are thought to be essential to the dramatic activity. Because individual and group development is encouraged, the general nature of the activity is non-competitive although some argue that in drama children compete strongly for attention. As in primary school education, there is a stress on learning through discovery and action. Children's own forms of expression are encouraged.

The general attitude to children, as found in the literature, is that teachers should work with children on the children's own levels. It is interesting that in most forms of drama mentioned – with the exception of theatre arts – *knowledge as content is not organised*. Subject matter is chosen because of the teacher's individual view of how children should develop; e.g. Dorothy Heathcote's emphasis on acting out social issues rather than using myth or fantasy. Because of this the status of knowledge is low although the method of learning is thought to be important.

More will be said about methodology (the presentation of knowledge, pupils' handling of content and types of evaluation) when types of teaching and learning have been described and discussed. It is, however, relevant to say that most approaches mentioned stress the importance of drawing on pupils' ideas and that the dramatic activity itself presupposes the notion of learning by action rather than by reading and writing. Group work is also important in drama. As with other types of progressive education, creativity and invention is encouraged. In none of the literature studied was any specific form of evaluation explicitly mentioned.

Because of the stress on development through play (by acting), interpersonal relations are stressed more than in more formal situations or in classes where individual development is thought to be most important.

From this it can be seen that most of the approaches to educational drama have characteristics similar to those of 'progressive' education, particularly the attitudes to knowledge, to children, the approaches to methodology and the stress on interpersonal relationships where children's subjective attitudes are recognised as important.

In one sense, therefore, drama in secondary schools could be said to be continuing the type of education that prevails in some primary schools. It does however focus on acting and is different inasmuch as the development of the group is thought to be as important as that of the individual.

The recent emergence of one of the approaches – 'theatre arts' – as an examination subject indicates, however, that the development of drama is a complicated matter. It is quite possible that to get established in an examination-dominated secondary system, the subject will have to adopt some of the features of traditional types of curriculum and therefore in some cases be less innovatory than the term 'educational drama' normally implies.

The intention of this brief account of some of the main concepts and assumptions found in drama teaching has been to indicate what most drama teachers have in common. An attempt has also been made to see how drama fits in with educational philosophies and ways of teaching as a whole. Within these general assumptions exist differences in intention and attitude. The deep divisions within the drama world have not served to promote the subject but rather to reinforce the idea that the present state of drama is muddled and that there are no firm theoretical foundations upon which to argue for the development of the subject in general.

In the next chapter I intend to describe some of the divisions that occur in drama (for instance, concerning the place of discussion in drama lessons, and whether children should or should not show their work) and to argue that the disagreements that occur are based on the false premise that there is only one way to teach drama. There are different emphases depending on how and what is taught. Often teachers use examples of poor practice as reasons for dismissing a particular type of drama without looking at the possibilities within each approach.

3 The controversial nature of drama

A brief account of the main debates found in drama teaching might serve to indicate the present state of theory of drama. The nature of the controversies highlights differences in opinion and practice. In some cases the types of arguments given indicate some of the confusion about the nature and function of drama found among teachers today. In this chapter I hope to show that disagreements occur not only through ideological differences, but also because teachers mistakenly use examples of poor work in a particular type of drama as valid reasons why that sort of drama ought not to be used. Many teachers fail to allow for the possibility that different approaches to drama involve the use of different kinds of activities.

There are two main areas of controversy at present. The first is concerned with whether drama teachers should allow students to perform in front of audiences. The other is about the place of discussion in drama lessons.

To show or not to show

In the early days of drama in schools, teachers were expected to teach 'speech and drama'. Drama teachers seemed to focus on two main things – presentation of scripted plays and use of the voice. Delivery/performance was emphasised. Pupils often learnt texts, prose and poetry off by heart, recited and performed them. This frequently resulted in stilted performances where children did not really understand the content of what they were reciting. They could, however, be heard, and had clear, resonant and precise diction. It is still possible to find sets of scripts and speech exercises tucked away in some schools.

On the positive side, pupils were in command of their voices and very often came to a greater appreciation of the work they were reciting. Those who went in for public speaking and poetry reading gained a great deal of confidence in their ability to control their voices and speak in front of audiences. These kinds of activities still go on and examples of good work can be found in festivals run by the Poetry Society and the English Speaking Board.

Teachers influenced by the 'method' type of acting reacted against this way of working. The emphasis, they felt, should be on what it is like to feel that you are a particular character. The actor's experience and the way he builds up pictures of the people and plays is what is important. External features of gesture and speech should come from the way in which the actor has internalised the character – what it means to him.

Many teachers feel that in the classroom, performance does not matter. It is the process of acting and exploring meaning through acting that is important. The educational significance is that the child learns through his own experience. They argue that if children feel that they should *show* their work, then they will concentrate on working towards 'show', rather than using drama as a means for exploration. This could mean that their work is often hurried or superficial and that they are self-conscious about acting in front of people. It is an opportunity for the extrovert to show off and could be damaging for the child who is shy and retiring. Teachers who concentrate on 'showing' often emphasise the performing skills, i.e. that the actors can be seen and heard, rather than the quality of the content children are portraying or on how the children's perceptions have changed as a result of the experience. Some teachers feel so strongly about this that they refuse to let children show their work to others.

On the opposite side of the picture are people who feel that educational drama, with all its emphasis on the experience of the child, is leading the child to a greater understanding of and participation in the theatre.

The following arguments could be used in favour of this attitude. Drama has been used effectively through the ages as an art form. Playwrights have expressed their understanding and views about human beings through plays. These insights have been communicated to audiences in theatres where they have sometimes been appreciated. Some new perceptions might have been gained from them. Students who attempt to communicate scripts to other people not only find more out about a playwright's intentions, but also have the experience of communicating with people on a different, more organised, level than they would otherwise do.

There is another argument for staging performances. It enables a great many people to work together at different levels – some acting, others behind the stage – and to produce something that is coordinated and complete at the end. Its impact is immediate and students are able to see and hear whether they have been successful. It is an effective means of demonstrating to people that they are capable of working towards and achieving goals. This could give the non-academic child a great deal of confidence.

The main problem lies in the quality of the work produced during performances. At its best it can provide moments of intensity, either humorous or serious, and give aesthetic pleasure if what is seen and heard is presented as a satisfying work of art. At its worst it can be 'chaotic'. Backstage effects can happen at the wrong time: sun when it's supposed to be raining; noises sounding at the wrong moments, or not at all – the telephone that never rings. Children can be embarrassed to appear in front of others. Lines may be forgotten or said in the wrong order. The plot of the play might be so slight that, apart from Mrs Brown's pleasure at seeing her son appearing on stage, the whole affair could be most embarrassing. Things are not usually as bad as this, but the quality is often mediocre and the performance unexciting. It is often the experience of such stage performances, poor both in content and acting, that puts some teachers off the whole notion of performance. This, however, does not deter those who feel that working towards performance has value for the reasons already given.

There are a number of teachers who take the 'child centred' approach (i.e. who believe in the importance of drama as a creative process for the child) but who also believe in children showing their work. This usually happens when groups of children are asked to create their own plays once the teacher has given them a stimulus. The children sometimes produce something they are pleased about. What they have constructed says what they want to say. Often they want to show this to others – usually their peers. In this case, teachers allow students to show their work. The content as well as presentation has been devised by the children and their work takes place in the context of the classroom which lacks the glamour of the theatre. The focus is on the end product and on how the children have achieved their scenes. Importance is attached to their understanding and portrayal of characters and situations in their own terms rather than in those of an outside playwright.

Another kind of drama where audiences are involved is where the teacher wants children to react to and demonstrate a particular aspect of behaviour, for example interview situations. A small number of children will be asked to do something in front of the others. Their reactions and ways of coping with particular types of situations will be discussed. It is the teacher's way of highlighting particular techniques of communication so that children can have an idea of how to cope with the same situation in reality. This kind of work often involves role play (where people play specific roles) or simulation (where situations are recreated and students play specific parts in the situations, e.g. a United Nations committee).

Some of the main arguments for and against the use of performance have been mentioned. I would argue that whether children do or do not perform depends on the teacher's intention and in some cases whether the time is appropriate for 'showing'. Children might not be ready for it. Many teachers who have criticised the performance aspects of drama have based their objections on examples of bad practice, and have refused to see that the activity could have some benefits as well. To insist on showing when an activity is purely exploratory would be to miss the point. However, when there is something to communicate to others that can best be done in dramatic form, it seems ridiculous not to allow children to perform.

The place of discussion in drama

Some drama lessons begin with a discussion about what the children are going to do in the lesson. They decide with the teacher on the story line and on who they are going to be, and begin to act it out. Throughout the lesson, they discuss their progress up to that point before continuing. An example of this could be a class of thirteen-year-olds being asked to provide an idea for play making. They say they would like to try something with robots. A discussion takes place in which they decide the robot is to be the teacher who is to take on an authoritarian role. He dictates every move they make. They begin. The teacher gives instructions. Action is stopped by the teacher who suggests that a group of them might undermine the authority of the robot. A discussion takes place as to whether this is possible given the situation they are acting in. They then discuss ways in which they might subvert the robot. They try it out. At the end of the lesson, there is a post mortem on how the story went, how they reacted to the imagined situation, and whether parallels could be drawn with similar situations in real life.

Sometimes these kinds of lessons contain more discussion than action. Teachers who believe that the value of drama lies in the actual process of working it out in action would argue that children sit around enough in other lessons. Discussions could occur during English lessons. It is also argued that this kind of work means that the children are working at a very low key. Because they stop and start, and reflect on what they are doing and what to do next, it is not very easy for them to become totally involved in the characters and situations they are working out. Characters often remain superficial and this kind of work seldom touches on the complexities of human relationships.

The kind of discussion just described takes place during the course of the lesson. An extreme example has been given, although it should be said that within every drama lesson some form of discussion normally takes place. The question is how much, for what purposes, and at what points in the lesson.

There are two other kinds of discussion which occur in drama lessons that some teachers have reservations about. One is when a particular aspect (usually social or historical) is explored in dramatic terms. This usually leads up to a discussion about the issues involved and means that a great deal of time is often spent on the teacher's comments on the subject. Pupils are invited to discuss the issues and give their opinions on them as well as indicate their grasp of the subject. This kind of lesson is used as a means of teaching about a particular topic, and is sometimes used by teachers who are not drama specialists.

The objection to using this kind of lesson as a service to other subjects is that it undermines the status of drama in its own right. Children's own creativity is channelled too narrowly along the lines of the topic. They do not have a great deal of freedom to explore characters and situations at their own level. Drama as a subject in its own right demands proficiency in a number of skills so that children are given the maximum opportunity to express their own ideas verbally, mentally and physically as well as possible.

The other kind of discussion some people object to is that which occurs after performances – either of work created by the children or performances of plays already written. Some teachers feel that every individual experiences a performance individually and that it is the personal impact that matters. If this is so, discussion could be irrelevant. Others feel that the good dramatic performance synthesises meaning on many levels – it gives portraits of characters; it deals with wider social issues; it gives off symbols which are expressed by the body and sound and lighting effects. To discuss aspects of the play would be to distort the overall meaning conveyed. One of the important ways audiences could be said to react to plays is emotionally. They feel empathy, antagonism, interest. Whatever it is, there is a certain kind of communication or emotional impact between actors and audience that might be destroyed by translating the play to a more cerebral level. People feel that sometimes the level of discussion is low, that teachers pinpoint the wrong things. For example, it is common for teachers, when looking at children's work, to criticise the way the children look and sound rather than discuss the quality of the work that the children have created – i.e. in terms of whether the play approximates to what they are trying to say, and how they might improve the characters or situations they portray. It is probably better to have no discussion than irrelevant discussion. This is because the way in which teachers criticise pupils' work sets standards of achievement for future work.

All these arguments are relevant to some kinds of work taking place in drama. There is often failure, however, to examine the reasons why certain kinds of discussion take place. This might have to do with pupils being at a particular stage of development and there being a need to focus on a particular issue in order to advance their work. It might be that teachers have specific intentions with regard to what they want children to get out of their work.

In the case where discussion is used to make decisions about progress or to discuss what has been going on, the teacher may want the pupils to feel more distanced about the activity than they otherwise would. It may be that he would like pupils to be conscious of the way in which decisions can be made. This might be a useful method of enabling children to be aware of how their work connects with decision taking in society. In general the technique, however, does not encourage many moments of emotional intensity or in-depth explorations of character. It might also be said that if there is a great deal of discussion, there is less opportunity for 'acting' as such, so that not much drama would take place in that kind of lesson.

When drama is used as a means to stimulate discussion about particular material, it has certain benefits. The use of acting in other subject areas gives an experiential dimension that reading or talking about it does not. It enables students to imagine what it would have been like to have been in a particular kind of situation. It also helps them, through their reactions in various situations, to fill in detail, and to be aware of the human implications. An example of this could be where children are considering the Ulster problem. They could be asked to represent various factions and then told to negotiate for a peace settlement. Facts about the situation could be fed in, but the actual experience of negotiating highlights the complexities and difficulties of coming to an amicable conclusion. It acts as a reminder to students that political decisions are made by people rather than things which merely appear as facts and arguments in books.

Because the focal point of this method is on understanding content, it does not develop the creativity of children as fully as it could do. As in any other art form, a long period of experimentation and work is needed before children can create end products of good quality. In this sense, work based on learning about content has its limitations.

If, in contrast to the method just described, the emphasis in discussion after performance is on what is being communicated and how it could best be put across (i.e. whether characters and situations could be believed in or not), then lack of discussion could be unproductive, as it would give pupils no indication of how they could improve their work in the future. Discussion is also necessary for the teacher so that he can find out how pupils arrived at their ideas, what their ideas and difficulties were, and how they could develop. In cases where general issues are being explored by pupils, for example, the question of authority, it might be useful to discuss the implications of the pupils' interpretations (for example, they might decide to murder an authoritarian character which might or might not be an appropriate solution to the problem posed).

It should now be clear that the point being made is that the part that discussion should play in drama cannot be a foregone conclusion. The type of discussion taking place and how long it lasts depends on what the pupils' and teacher's intentions are and on the kind of drama in question. Some forms of drama lend themselves more to discussion than others. It should be said, however, that unless discussion takes place within a dramatic situation, that discussion could not be said to be 'drama' as no acting takes place. A lesson in which only discussion occurred could not be termed a drama lesson. When there is discussion, attention should be given to the relevance of what is being discussed and the quality of the discussion itself.

In this chapter I have mentioned two main areas of controversy in drama teaching. Attempts have been made to show that arguments for and against the value of different kinds of drama practices are often based on confused thinking. Teachers cite examples of bad practice as justifications for not using, for example, performance or discussion, rather than looking at the reasons why certain kinds of practices are employed. It would be better to look at ways of teaching in terms of what their advantages and disadvantages are for teachers and their pupils.

The standpoints of different approaches to drama have been touched upon in this chapter. What has not been done yet is to show how these approaches actually work in practice and what methods are used in teaching drama in various ways.

Part II will describe some of the activities used in varying degrees by most drama teachers, regardless of what their particular emphasis might be. Detailed case studies of the most common ways of working in drama will follow. Readers will be able to see how teachers tackle drama with particular reference to the kind of children they teach and the kinds of school they teach in. These case studies will also serve to illustrate some of the general points already made.

PART II

Drama teaching in practice

Introduction

So far discussions about what drama is and can do have been conducted in the abstract. This section will deal with some of the most common forms of drama taught in the classroom. It will give examples of the work of five teachers who have different approaches to teaching the subject. These different descriptions will make it possible to see how drama is taught in the context of the school and to understand the special needs of particular kinds of pupils.

Each case study will indicate how certain methods can be taught. Generalisations will be drawn, from the examples given, of the kinds of achievements certain methods of teaching could produce.

Differences will be discussed in the light of the main variables which appear to influence outcomes in drama teaching. These include differences in the teacher's aims and intentions, the content he has chosen, whether a pupil's work is directed or undirected and the size of the groups involved in the lesson. These variables largely determine the nature of the contribution that children will be able to make in a lesson.

Each case study will therefore include the following:

1 A general picture of the school and the particular pupils discussed.
2 The teacher's attitudes, aims and intentions.
3 Descriptions of work done with pupils, either in terms of sequences of lessons or descriptions of whole lessons where relevant.

4 Descriptions of any kinds of development observed in lessons.
5 General comments about the usefulness of working in certain ways.

Five distinctive ways of working will be described:

1 The use of movement and formal mime in drama.
2 Teacher directed whole group drama where some role play is used.
3 Child centred group improvisations.
4 The use of drama as a service subject.
5 Drama as training for the theatre.

Examples have deliberately been taken from different types of schools, ability and age ranges to indicate that drama can be taught to all kinds of pupils.

Clearcut differences in teaching methods have been described in order to show that there are a variety of ways in which drama can be taught. It is however important to state that many teachers try out different methods depending on the needs of their pupils and what their particular interests at a given time will be.

Because some of the concepts that drama teachers have are basic to the subject (as described earlier in the book), some of the activities involved in drama are used by most teachers. For instance, two teachers with different approaches to drama may both use movement or games to start a lesson. This is because they both believe in the development of physical or verbal skills in furthering their aims. Part II will therefore deal not only with differences found in drama, but also with those aspects which most drama lessons or series of drama lessons have in common.

4 The use of movement and formal mime in drama

Drama can be of value in both academic and non-academic schools. I have used work in a particular grammar school to indicate ways in which drama can be used to complement the more formal aspects of children's education.

A general picture of the school and pupils

The school is a small urban grammar school in a pleasant residential area. There are 750 boys. They come from within the top ability groups and are divided into subject groups. All pupils are expected to work towards A levels and are expected to go on to some form of higher education when they leave school – mainly university. Most of the boys come from professional families but there are also some whose parents are skilled workers, e.g. telephone engineers. Uniform is common. The cadet force is popular in the school. The atmosphere tends to be traditional and formal. Boys are normally addressed by their surnames.

There is no drama department. One English teacher is officially in charge of oral English examinations and of producing the school play. He teaches drama as part of his English lessons. Some members of the English department under his guidance have tried some drama with varying success. No drama is timetabled. The only classes receiving regular drama are those taught by the teacher and his pupils have drama for one year only because he then changes classes.

There is a special drama studio paid for in part from funds raised from performances, the P.T.A. and the school.

The headmaster does not approve of the subject and the majority of staff are sceptical about it although they are proud of the reputation that the school has for public performances.

The pupils observed

There were thirty boys aged thirteen in the class. When they first began drama they thought they were wasting their time. 'Drama doesn't teach you anything.'

They learnt drama in a 'drama room' which consisted of a large empty room containing a few chairs and a table. The room had recently been converted to a studio with a new floor and white walls. Windows lined one side giving an impression of space and light.

The teacher's attitudes and aims

As far as the teacher was concerned, the boys in this school were articulate and intelligent, but found difficulty in expressing themselves physically. This was because they were self-conscious and rather wooden in movement. He felt that if they had more command over their bodies and could express themselves physically, they would, on the one hand, be more spontaneous, and on the other hand, have enough confidence to put across what they wanted. For these reasons he felt that he should concentrate on the physical aspects of drama and thought that for these boys, because of their formal training, formal mime – i.e. the use of clearly defined accepted traditional gestures – would be a good place to start. He also felt that the type of informal movement which encouraged exploration of space, control of the body and physical contact between students was useful because it encouraged boys to work together on a more basic level than that to which they were accustomed.

The teacher felt that this class lacked self-discipline and concentration and found it difficult to work together.

General methods used

FIRST TERM

Most of the teacher's lessons at the beginning of the year were concerned with teaching the boys a number of formal mime routines, for example opening a door, feeling along a wall, defining various objects. The emphasis was on how clearly boys could physically create the illusions of imaginary objects. They were trained to be sensitive to the physical properties of objects – size, shape, heaviness, differences in heat and texture. The teacher therefore emphasised the acquisition of miming skills, concentrating on clarity of gesture in the first term.

Lessons consisted of the teacher demonstrating an example of a mime technique and explaining the movements as he went along, for example the use of the neutral spread hand to indicate that a particular movement was ended. The boys then copied him until they got the movement right. They were then asked to work in groups to devise sequences of movements in which the particular mime featured. For instance they would be asked to form a sequence in which opening a window, drinking a hot drink and climbing stairs occurred. Each group's work was then discussed in terms of the accuracy of the work produced. The teacher did, however, sometimes vary the mode of these lessons. For instance he had boys working in pairs mirroring each other's actions, or groups balanced against each other or pushing and pulling each other. He often played games (for instance, murder) at the end of lessons or when he thought they needed a rest. He sometimes used speech (for instance, story telling around a circle) and some group improvisations involving speech, but most of his work was physical.

SECOND AND THIRD TERMS

Work in the last two terms was of a similar nature and differed inasmuch as more time was given to boys to work on their own and the size of groups changed.

It was only after the boys had acquired a repertoire of movements that they were meant to use them in the expression of ideas. This was done in one of two ways. In the first half of the second term, the boys worked as a class on the story of Theseus in which they mimed various sequences of the story. Normally, however, the teacher gave the boys topics to work on. These ranged from abstract notions of being hunted to being given a number of objects as stimuli for making scenes.

Examples of lessons showing the development of one group of boys over the year

I have used the work of one group of boys to illustrate the kind of development that this type of drama work can achieve. Brief descriptions of lessons in each term will be given showing how the group tackled the problems given.

TERM ONE: VARIATIONS ON OPENING A DOOR

The group observed were of average ability in their class. They picked up the movements fairly quickly and after a few weeks mastered some basic techniques – this appeared to give them some satisfaction and they started experimenting on their own.

The teacher started the particular lesson described by reminding them of the technique of opening a door. He then asked the boys to work out a scene using the movements they had learnt. He gave the group about twenty minutes to work something out.

The group started work as soon as the teacher let them. There were no quarrels about roles and as soon as they decided on the theme – 'let's do something about a salesman' – they started practising, using trial and error, rejecting ideas as they went along. Each boy participated by suggesting something. Their scene started with an old man coming in with his son. They were arguing. In mock politeness the son opened the door for the old man. In his turn, the man gestured to his son to go first. Meanwhile, one of the boys, walking around with tennis balls up his jumper to show femininity, opened the door and the two others went in. The fourth boy came up to the door carrying a case. He knocked on the door. When the old man opened it, he stuck his foot in the door and started showing the contents of the case. The old man slammed the door and the salesman went off limping.

In this scene, most of the movements were clear. The audience knew exactly what was happening. The characters however were crude – for example, one knew that the man was old because he hobbled, and that the son was cross because he wagged his fingers. By the end of the term this group were capable of putting more detail into their scenes, were precise about their gestures and had the beginnings of characterisation – they were starting to respond to characters as if they were real people.

TERM TWO: THEME OF RESCUING

In this lesson the boys were merely given the idea of someone needing to be rescued. They were allowed a little speech and were given forty minutes to work something out. By the end of this lesson (halfway through the second part of the term) the boys had developed a great deal.

There was improvement in characterisation and the actual miming movements were more detailed and inventive. It took the boys less time to work out their scenes and they spent more time in practising their final decisions; i.e. polishing their final scene.

Their final scene consisted of three boys coming into a restaurant and sitting down and looking at the menu. This was done with a lot of miming and a little speech. A typical Italian waiter with exaggerated gestures and accent took the orders. He brought the food balanced on a tray and laid it down with evident pride. The boys started with very hot soup and from the expressions on their faces it was evident they didn't like it. Pizzas then arrived with the waiter saying it was the chef's special. They tried to eat it, but found it so hard they couldn't cut it. They were rescued by a boy miming a dog coming under the table and taking the pizza. The dog was so disgusted that he weed on it. The waiter ran after the dog, shouting at the clients. They were so furious they threw the pizza in the waiter's face. The scene ended with him wiping it off.

By this time the rest of the class were rolling about with laughter. Not only was the demonstration done with more confidence than in the first term, but the objects were portrayed in more detail. For instance, the tray was round and heavy; there was more detail when the boys ate – from one boy dusting his chair before he sat down, to another unfolding a napkin before eating. The menu retained its shape and size as it was passed around and all boys pointed to the same spot on the menu when ordering.

Each boy had a different character. One was positive and looked forward to enjoying his meal. Another was nervous and didn't like Italian food. Another didn't want to spend a lot of money. They all interacted with each other in character and all had different reactions to tasting their dishes even though they all disliked what they had.

TERM THREE: WORK ON AN OBJECT WITH CHANGING QUALITIES

The teacher started the lesson with the boys in a circle holding imaginary objects and then changing the size of the objects. He then asked them to change the object in such a way that it was clear to an onlooker. As soon as the boys got the idea, he sent them away in groups to work on a scene in which one object changed as many times as the boys wanted.

The group started with an imaginary cat and changed it into six different animals – progressing in size to an elephant and then diminishing to a poisonous spider. Miming was detailed, but the boys started the work by saying that they wanted their objects to mean something. One boy suggested that they explore a theme through it. After some discussion they decided on the theme of fear. There was some debate about what fear really was. One boy thought you can be scared of something, but it isn't really anything that is dangerous. Another said that 'often you're really frightened about something what's really big, like a shadow, and not scared of something small'. One boy replied 'Yeah. And something small could be really lethal – like a pill'.

They then tried a number of ways in which these ideas could be expressed, including agoraphobia, poisoning and fear of examinations. Eventually they hit on the idea that different attitudes to types of animals could express their ideas. For instance, they showed initial fear of the elephant which changed to respect. They showed no fear of the spider, letting it run over their hands until at the end of the scene one of them was bitten and died. This was done in total silence.

The main development for this group in the third term was that the group were interested in giving some form of symbolic significance to their work. The amount of discussion about the subject increased rather than there being more discussion about the sequence of events or characters. This was probably due to the type of topic which their teacher gave them to work on which was of an abstract rather than concrete nature.

THE GROUP'S ACHIEVEMENT

This group was fairly successful compared to the rest of the class. Some boys found it difficult to develop a complete command of mime by the end of the year so that some of their movements were so generalised that it was difficult to see what they were doing. This class's main achievement was physical with an emphasis on the attainment and use of certain formal miming techniques. At the beginning of the year almost all the boys were stiff, self-conscious and wooden when expressing themselves. Not only did they become more self-confident and relaxed through movement training, but the actual range of expression increased. Movements became clearer, less generalised and more detailed. This showed that the boys remembered perceptions of physical objects and they became more accurate. In addition, there was a general improvement in group participation, concentration and the ability to create and understand characters and situations. They were also more able to shape their ideas into some kind of meaningful form and to put their ideas across clearly and effectively. Their attitude, with the exception of about four boys, changed from being sceptical to exploratory although, when I interviewed some of them at the end of the year, they still questioned the value of drama.

Comments

This case study was an attempt to show how drama can profitably be used in schools where the emphasis is on formal schooling. In a school where much of the activity is sedentary, drama using movement and mime can help children relax more, give them more physical control and the ability to express their feelings and thoughts with more self-confidence. At a time when the importance of 'body language' is being mentioned by people as an effective form of communication in addition to that of speech, it would be a pity to deny children a training that gives them scope to express themselves and to communicate in more ways than one.

This teacher used mime for these particular boys because he felt that they would be more willing to attempt this more formal study of movement rather than the Laban type of movement which encourages a great deal of free expression. Once the boys were able to gain physical confidence by perfecting mime techniques, they were able to use these techniques as a secure basis for self-expression. Drama gave them a means of working and problem solving different from that to which they were normally accustomed.

In observing these boys' lessons over a week, it became evident, even in art lessons, that the emphasis was on learning how to analyse, understand and cope with subject matter. They had well developed mental faculties, were able to comprehend written work well and to articulate their understanding of subjects. When they gave their opinions (for example, on a historical event) they were encouraged to be as objective as possible and to give rational reasons for their decisions. In drama they were given a freer hand to express things that were of subjective importance to them, e.g. the fact that they were frightened of size rather than realising that danger can come in all forms. Once they had acquired mime techniques, they were left to devise scenes which expressed the ideas they had formulated. These did not come from a given body of knowledge. The boys had to use their own internal resources and images to form the structures of the plays they made. In addition they needed to work in groups rather than on their own. In the classroom (with the exception of the music lesson), they almost always worked on their own. Drama therefore gave them the opportunity of working constructively with other boys. At first they found this difficult because they were continually looking for a competitive element in their work and asked when they were going to be examined. After a while most of them realised that they were working differently. In this case, therefore, drama lessons gave the boys the chance to be creative in their own right, to learn to express themselves with more confidence, more inventiveness and more physical control, to learn about a particular kind of technique sometimes used in drama, and how to be creative in the dramatic form.

The general uses of movement and mime in drama

This case study indicates one way in which mime can be used to form the basis of dramatic activity. Movement in various forms (which incorporates both informal and formal ways of moving) is extensively used in drama lessons. All the teachers mentioned in the book have used movement in one form or another.

Movement can achieve three main things. First, it helps to improve a child's physical coordination and control and gives children a wider physical vocabulary for expressing themselves. Secondly, it makes people much more aware of their physical environment, and in particular of qualities of speed, space, shape, size and texture. Thirdly, with some forms of movement, children are helped to work more cooperatively through the use of physical contact and trust exercises (e.g. where a particular balancing exercise will not work unless the person balanced trusts the other to support him).

In this case study mime was emphasised. It might therefore be useful to look at how other forms of movement can be used in drama classes.

Sometimes a drama teacher will start the lesson with general relaxation exercises – children are asked to lie down and clench and relax certain parts of their bodies. This often puts them into a state of readiness to start working.

Children may be asked to move around the room in different ways, or to create various movement sequences. Here children are often encouraged to use as much variety of movement as possible – working with different parts of the body at different levels or speeds, for example. They are sometimes asked to make various shapes with their bodies which can represent emotional states or abstract ideas – 'I want you to make a shape with your body that shows you are very cold and hungry'. This kind of movement helps children to be aware of their bodies. It means that when they want to express themselves in drama they are more able to use the most appropriate physical form and to make the most effective use of the space they have been given.

Often combined with this is movement work which is done in pairs or groups in which people work together on a particular movement. For example, one child will be asked to devise a set of movements that his partner will mirror. This requires, on the one hand, a recognition of the right kinds of movement – not too complicated for a partner to follow; and on the other hand, accuracy of perception in order to copy the other's movements. There is often physical contact – pushing and pulling and balancing, or merely leading someone blindfolded in a room. These forms of movement could serve to build up trust in people and allow them to be sensitive to and react to the capabilities of their fellow workers.

Children are frequently helped to become imaginatively involved in the situations they enact by being asked to pretend that they are in a particular physical environment. They are asked physically to plot out the objects, e.g. beds and chairs, in the places they are in and to pretend that they are doing certain things in that space, e.g. washing, getting dressed etc. – all in silence. Usually the teacher talks them through these activities, asking them to think about the details of the objects they are imagining, e.g. shape and size. This helps them to concentrate on the situations they are working on because they are more able to see the scenes in physical and visual settings.

A mixture of different kinds of movements may be used, depending on what the teacher wants to achieve at a certain time. It could, however, be generally said that all forms of movement training, including mime, encourage improved physical expression, physical control and coordination and can be used as a basis for creative work. This training is useful both for the child who generally verbalises in order to communicate and for the child whose main form of expression is physical.

This chapter has described how children could benefit from a training in movement and mime, especially if their general education is academic. The more general discussion concerning the uses of movement and mime was given to illustrate the educational value of these ways of working.

5 Teacher directed drama with the class as a whole

A general picture of the school and pupils

This school is very different from the grammar school of the last chapter. It is a comprehensive school consisting of 1,300 pupils. It is co-educational and has a predominantly working class intake. There are three bands in the first three years: three classes in the top range ability, three in the middle, and three remedial forms. There is a large sixth form with pupils who are mainly doing C.S.E. and some O levels. Parents' occupations range from working on the buses to owning small shops. The area consists of a mixture of council flats and run down Victorian houses. The school is a large expanse of grey concrete buildings with a rather oppressive atmosphere. The children do not wear uniform.

The school has a drama department consisting of a head of department and three other specialist drama teachers – two also teach English and one specialises in dance. All classes in the first three years are timetabled for drama. The remedial classes have more drama than other classes. There is an optional C.S.E. course in the fourth and fifth years. There are school performances of some sort almost every term.

From interviews with the head, deputy head and other teachers, there seemed to be a general emphasis on compensatory education. They all saw the school as providing an alternative environment for pupils coming from physically and culturally deprived homes, which gave them access to cultural experiences that would otherwise be denied them.

The headmaster supported drama and felt that it improved behaviour. 'You know, generally speaking, our school is a relaxed school and I do attribute this to the amount of drama activity we have . . . it does allow them to develop their personalities and gives them more understanding of other people.' Most members of the staff supported the subject although many did not know what it involved.

Despite this, it is interesting to note that the drama budget was a fifth of that spent on improving facilities for A level science students, of whom there were less than five at that time.

The pupils

The class studied was a second year remedial class. This means that they were rated as below average in a school which did not have a full ability quota to begin with. There were twenty children.

When I first saw the pupils, the teacher had not yet come into the room. The boys sat in one straight row and the girls sat opposite them. My first impression was one of shabbiness, i.e. patched blazers, thinning, shining trousers. The girls wore clogs with stubbed toes and plastic baubles in their hair. The pupils seemed subdued, almost sullen and hardly took any notice of me. One boy was wandering aimlessly around the room opening lockers, taking books out and throwing them on the floor. He was ignored by other pupils. There were vast differences in the children's feelings about drama, which were based on their assumption that drama taught you to be an actor. Those keen on being actors and actresses liked it. The others felt it was a waste of time and about a third of the boys refused to do it for one and a half terms.

The state of the classroom did not help matters. The room was long and some of the walls were peeling. The children said it was too hot in summer and too cold in winter.

The teacher's attitude and aims

The teacher felt that most of the children had problems. He pointed out one boy who had very slight brain damage. Another boy was on the borderline of being educationally subnormal. He showed me a small Chinese boy who spoke no English. When he addressed the pupils, he spoke slowly, clearly and gave simple statements and instructions. On the whole the pupils reacted calmly and respectfully and called him 'Sir'. Except for cases when a child disrupted the whole class, he generally allowed pupils to participate or not as they chose. In this way he contained the more hostile elements in the class. This tied in with one of his main aims – that pupils should be given the maximum opportunity to make choices.

This was bound up with his feeling that most other subjects did not give the child such an opportunity, nor indeed the opportunity to develop along his own lines. 'I think eventually they've got to stand on their own two feet.' If the teacher gave a group of children an idea and left them to use it as they wanted, then this was a good thing. Success in drama 'comes when a group completely takes off from you – when they are on their own'.

He believed that drama was a useful subject in which to prepare for the future. 'Give them experience of what might lie in the future for them. Drama ought to give the kid the chance to explore something he may come across in real life.'

He felt that what children do in drama should depend on their particular needs at any one time. This was why in the third term he switched his teaching from an undirected method to a more directed method.

I intend to describe the third term's work to show how a form of teacher directed drama can be of use to children who find it difficult to work creatively on their own.

Before I discuss the third term's work, however, it might be useful to provide an impression of the teacher's work as a whole so that the third term can be seen in perspective.

Brief account of methods used over the year

Lessons followed a similar pattern in the first two terms. He often began with games – usually word games – and then worked mainly with small groups. He had hoped to do some movement but found the room too small. Lessons were structured so that the pupils had concrete things to do – for example, in one lesson he set up an imaginary T.V. studio with cameras, microphones, sets, etc., in other lessons he gave them job interviews to do or taught them specific skills, e.g. how to throw a custard pie effectively. The most common form of lesson was to give pupils a general stimulus and ask them to work out scenes around it. For example, he gave each group a number of hats and asked them to create their own characters and scenes out of them, or he asked them to make up their own advertisements; or played a record of Victorian sounds from which they were expected to build scenes. Lessons did not normally follow on from each other and were often interrupted when he was called out to attend rehearsals for performances the school was putting on.

Development among the pupils in the first two terms was unequal. This was due to hostile relationships between the boys and girls and their different attitudes towards the subject. The girls were enthusiastic, got on with their work and at the end of the two terms were able to produce well formulated plays in which the characters were interesting. For instance, the scene they developed from Victorian sounds was about the problems of an authoritarian father and the feelings of violence he provoked in his daughters. One group of boys had ambivalent feelings about drama and sometimes took part and sometimes did not. When they did join in they fought among themselves for parts and never got beyond the trial and error stages of trying out improvisations. The other group of boys refused to do drama at all and spent the first two terms reading or playing cards. This was allowed by the teacher as they did not disrupt other people's work and by the end of the second term, when the other pupils were beginning to produce work of reasonable quality, they were beginning to get interested in attempting something themselves. They were thus willing to participate when the teacher tried to get the whole class to work together in the third term.

By that time he felt that although the girls were capable of making choices, the boys – and especially the class as a whole – 'were not capable of working on their own. They're not quite ready to do that as a whole group. Relationships have to be very good to do that'.

Work in the third term. Whole class work where the teacher plays a role

The teacher used the theme of travelling to another country as a basis for work in this term. He began the series of lessons by asking pupils to act being in a travel agent's:

In your groups find a travel agent and the rest of you are going to be the person who wants to go away somewhere. Maybe you don't know where you want to go. You know what you want to do and how long to spend. I want the travel agent to sell you a holiday. He must take down all the details and be as helpful as possible.

He gave the most reluctant boys the roles of travel agent, set up physical offices for them, gave them sheets of paper and concrete instructions. The girls worked a story around their theme. The interesting thing is that all the boys took part. It seemed that they felt secure enough to suspend belief. This might have been because they felt the subject was relevant as it approximated to a real life situation. Although they enjoyed what they were doing and were involved in it, most of the time was spent arguing in role as to where they were going to go.

Because the atmosphere was a working one, the teacher felt he could try to get the boys and girls to work together without too much trouble. At the end of the lesson he called the class together and asked them what they had done and where they had decided to go. The conversation was animated and there was a great deal of discussion about what was best value for money when you could not afford a great holiday. The teacher suggested that they worked on going on holiday as a group the following lesson and asked them as a group to decide where they would like to go, and who they would like to be. After a great deal of argument they decided that they wanted to go to Italy and that they wanted to go as individuals on a chartered flight.

In the next lesson, the teacher asked the most reluctant boys if they could use chairs to set up the aeroplane. This they did with great enjoyment. He then asked the class where they would like to start.

The girls suggested starting from home. Most of the children got into bed and the teacher talked them through the procedure of getting up, having breakfast, packing and getting papers ready. It was interesting to see that the girls immediately assumed different characters whereas the boys acted themselves. Every member of the class was involved. The teacher warned them that the travel agent would be phoning to confirm the departure time.

The class continued to get ready. The teacher asked two boys to be pilot and co-pilot. They set up control units. He asked two other boys (the most disruptive) to be passport officers. They set up a table and chairs and improvised rubber stamps.

The phone rang and the rest of the class were told to proceed to the checking-in point. The teacher acted as a travel agent and guide. He took names, answered queries and gave them instructions about what to do next. When they got to the passport control the two boys took pleasure in stopping each child, questioning him about his destination and how much money he had. One boy had forgotten his passport. There was great consternation. Eventually one of the passport officers persuaded the pilot to hold up the plane while the boy went to get his passport. This was the first time that these particular boys were involved in any kind of dramatic activity. When it came to boarding the plane, however, they refused to get in, saying that they were passport men. The teacher asked them to change roles and to set up the welcoming hotel for the passengers when they arrived. They spent the rest of the lesson setting up tables and chairs, polishing imaginary glasses etc. This was the longest period of sustained involvement that these boys had achieved so far.

The rest of the class boarded the plane. Apart from the travel agent telling them about the type of hotel and place they were going to and where they could change their travellers' cheques, and the pilot (a rather shy boy) telling them about their flight and the importance of putting on safety belts, the rest of the journey was taken up with passengers relating with each other. Boys and girls actually reacted to each other in character for the first time. For example, two girls playing a fussy mother and reluctant teenage daughter sat in front of two boys playing tough. The boys started chatting up the girl. The girl told them to stop. The mother made a fuss and called a hostess. Eventually the boys were made to move.

In this lesson the general quality of imaginative involvement showed improvement. An increasing amount of detail was portrayed during the lesson. Instead of making their usual generalised gestures which indicated lack of interest, they were clear about what they were doing and their gestures of, for example, fastening seat belts, drinking fizzy drinks and eating hamburgers were precise and detailed. Members of the class started working with people they would have ignored before.

The final lesson of the series showed that the class as a whole was beginning to work on its own although the teacher needed to step in at times, in role, to stop the lesson getting out of hand. It began with the class arriving at the hotel and being welcomed by the two boys who told the group what the conditions were. There were complaints about the time that they were expected to be back at night. The teacher then told them that before they went to their rooms he was going to tell them about an incident that had really happened to a member of a school party going abroad. A schoolboy had come in drunk and had created a great deal of trouble resulting in his being sent home. He warned the group that if anything happened in this hotel it would have 'dire consequences' not only for the person concerned, but also for the whole party.

The idea was taken up and when the children had finished dinner – either complaining about or praising the spaghetti or miming having difficulties in eating it – most of them went to bed. Inevitably two boys came in drunk and went into the girls' bedroom by mistake. A scene evolved when a sober friend tried to get them out of the room. A girl woke up, started screaming, called the hotel manager who chased the drunk boys round the room. Chaos followed until the teacher intervened as the travel agent, hauled the boys out of the room and apologised to the hotel manager. The hotel manager (a boy who had previously refused to do drama) complained but said that if he could be compensated for the trouble caused he would overlook the boys' behaviour. After a great deal of bargaining, he accepted an amount of money and the lesson ended with everybody spontaneously deciding to go back to sleep. At the end of the lesson they said that they had enjoyed this lesson more than others because they had all worked together.

Comments

This example of teacher directed activity in which the teacher role plays can be used when children are unable to work profitably with other children or on their own. In this case the method gave a number of boys a safe structure in which to work. By involving the whole class, the more timid children were able to gain confidence in a way they probably could not on their own. The subject, too, was well chosen since it was probably of relevance to the children, and enabled them to practise going through some of the formalities of travelling. This structure was clearly defined. It was in a definite place with a definite purpose; some children were able for the first time to imagine what it would be like to be in an 'as if' situation. This was shown by the detail of their movements – e.g. fastening safety belts. It also meant that they could start experimenting with their action and therefore begin to invent; for instance, a scene might be created by a child spilling an imaginary glass of beer.

For the children, especially the girls, who were reasonably advanced in drama, the main asset was that in the class context they were given a chance to communicate in a constructive manner with the boys. In a class where there was such a feud between the sexes that none would talk to each other, this was a considerable advancement.

The general uses of teacher directed whole group activity where role play is used

The use of this kind of method need not necessarily be limited to children who find drama difficult and therefore need a safe environment in which to work. It can also be used for other purposes. Teacher directed role play can be used to teach history, for example. The teacher sets up a simulation (attempts to recreate a scene from records) and tightly structures the scene so that the relevant facts or features are fed in. In this way children could experience what it might have been like to have lived in a particular period.

The method can also be effectively used for play making by the group as a whole, with the teacher encouraging corporate decision-making about the next step of the plot. This is usually done by discussion: 'What shall we do next? Where do we go from here?' Often the teacher has a general theme or problem which he wants solved or explored and uses the children's ideas to do this. By role playing a character in the plot, he can focus on the theme he wants explored. For example, the children devise a story which is generally agreed by the whole class about a small group of mad scientists who have devised a lethal weapon and plan to use it. They had kept the weapon a secret. The teacher is interested in how ways can be found to discover secrets. He therefore role plays one of the scientists, who drops hints in such a way that members of the class have to investigate what he is saying. At the end of the lesson there is usually a discussion about why, for instance, people want to keep secrets from other people, which might include the official secrets act and whether the children think this is a good thing or not.

The ways of using teacher directed drama described above show that the teacher is important in structuring the framework of the lesson. This can be useful for children who need security before trying drama on their own, or can be used when the teacher has a specific purpose in mind, for instance, learning how corporate large group decisions are made.

6 Child centred group improvisations

General picture of the school

There are 1,200 pupils. The intake is fully comprehensive, both from the point of view of ability and in terms of social mix. Classes are unstreamed in the first three years, except for French, German, maths, science and Latin. There is a large sixth form with about a third doing A levels. Parents' occupations range from long distance lorry drivers to members of Parliament. The school is housed in three buildings – two brick and one concrete – with many windows and wood giving an impression of light. There is no uniform.

There is no drama department but a person in charge of drama within the English department. Three other English teachers also teach drama and it is left to the discretion of the particular teacher as to whether he or she wishes to teach drama. This means that most classes in the first three years have some drama, but this varies from class to class. There is a fourth and fifth form optional class which does not lead to any examination. There are no special facilities for drama at present, but a studio is now being built and a teacher has been offered a graded post for being in charge of drama.

According to the school's brochure, the main educational aim is 'the development of the individual' – or 'educating the child to do his own thing' as one head of house put it. The head also mentioned individual development.

Attitudes about drama varied from teachers thinking that 'It's really a bit of light relief from other subjects', 'It's dangerous. Just look at the state of classes coming from drama to other lessons', 'They're (drama teachers) impossible'; to 'It teaches them to express themselves and speak properly' and 'It's a good form of art like music and art'. Few of the teachers considered drama important enough to include in the school syllabus and one teacher thought that time and money spent on drama could have been spent on better things. One or two of them mentioned school performances but did not attach much importance to them.

The pupils

A second year mixed ability class was studied. There were thirty children. They had had the same teacher for two years who taught them English as well as drama.

On my first visit, almost all the pupils, with the exception of two girls who wore long skirts, wore the same clothes, i.e. jeans, jersey and plimsoles. In some cases it was difficult to tell the child's sex. The children all rushed in, ran around the hall and then started a game of statues.

When the teacher entered and clapped her hands, there was instant silence. They then played the game of 'sharks', which she led with great energy and obvious pleasure. ('Sharks' involves words being shouted, which require immediate physical response. The slowest child is eliminated from the game each time until one child is left.) The impression given was one of busy enjoyment.

In general, most pupils thought about the subject in positive terms and felt that it naturally followed on from English, ' 'cause you can act out what you write or talk about in English'.

Physical environment of drama room

This was a large gymnasium situated above the swimming pool so that every now and then echoes from the pool could be heard. It had a highly polished floor and the walls were covered with wall bars and ropes which the pupils sometimes climbed and often used as props during drama. Because the gym was so large, in winter it was often cold and pupils had to work with their coats on. Its size, however, enabled groups to work on their own with the minimum of interference. There were a few benches which were occasionally used but usually pupils sat in a semicircle round the teacher who also sat on the floor.

The teacher's attitudes and aims

Her attitude to the class was that it was good and lively, hard working and had 'some strong characters in it'. She also thought that the children as a class had a strong sense of humour and worked well in their groups. Her main regret was that in the first few terms the boys and girls worked separately.

Observation showed that she often explained things to the pupils, for example:

What I want you to do is to remember the reason why we do drama. It's to see if we can get on as a group, not only talk to each other, but listen. . . . I will be mentioning these two words all the time – control and concentration. Why is that? Control – if we want what we are doing to be good, we need control. Every part of the body and the mind must have control. Concentration – if we want to go deeply into things we need to concentrate.

She emphasised two main forms of development in drama: *social development* and *imaginative involvement*. The following quotes sum up her attitude.

SOCIAL DEVELOPMENT

I think the most important factor in terms of education is the social aspect. More than anything else. That's how I see it geared. They sit in their desks and they do maths – they write and listen and do what they are asked and they don't have to *work* and they don't have to *give* any ideas and have to share and they don't have three minutes to produce something. O.K., you know, they might be asked to write an essay, but it's just *there* and there's no way of participating. But, you know, if it wasn't on the timetable as drama, it would be lacking. Getting together to create something. Listening to other people – *caring* what another person has got to say. I think that is the most important thing.

IMAGINATIVE INVOLVEMENT

I think the involvement side of it is important too, because at that age – the first, second and third years at any rate – their imaginations are such that they can immerse and involve themselves in something and it surprises me because . . . when I hear the kids still talking in the corridor – what they were doing – I can't really believe that they were so involved and . . . I feel that just must be good.

She discussed ways in which drama could develop. For instance, she suggested that one could start with movement to get the groups together and also that, through movement, the children could become imaginatively involved in small physical details. (I have called this imaginative mime.) Movement was useful because it was 'without any barrier of a new word or an idea'. '. . . and then through that sort of thing you can gradually introduce them . . . to situations and then . . . work on characters'. Initial work on improvisation was 'to get their minds working on working the story up – really that's all that matters and then how quickly they can do it together'. If the characters were portrayed as caricatures at that stage, it did not matter too much. At a later stage 'I ask them to think quite deeply about the person they're trying out. They should have reached the stage where they have become more observant and watch people more closely'. She saw different methods as representing definite stages of development: movement (emphasis on individuals – situational direction by the teacher) to group involvement in working out stories to sensitivity to people and situations through detailed characterisation.

She did, however, change her emphasis after attending a course at the end of the second term. 'I have changed quite a lot, I think. I think issues are more important, and discussion too.'

Brief account of methods used by the teacher

Although the emphasis was on working with the class as a whole, the teacher also encouraged individual work, i.e. asking each pupil to work on his own to construct an imaginary environment, as well as working with pairs and in groups. Most of this type of work was used to build up to the class working together. The first term was very much oriented towards social events. The main pattern of the lesson was directed by her although characters and groups were expected to make contributions within the pattern.

In the first term she combined English and drama. She began by reading extracts from *Akenfield* to the pupils during English, and from there she encouraged each pupil to construct for himself a character in a fictitious village. They wrote diaries, drew maps and pictures etc. In drama lessons, they enacted the roles of the characters they created and became involved in a number of social events such as picnics, bonfires and an election. Some pupils wrote and gave election speeches which were discussed by members of the village who then elected a candidate.

The second term involved a mixture of class work (for example, they did the story of Jason) and small group work on topics such as 'The worst day of my life' and 'Teenage conflict situation'. Pupils were often allowed to form their own groups which were strictly according to sex. At the end of the second term the teacher had a long talk with the pupils, trying to convince them that the sexes ought to mix.

In the third term, they asked to be divided into mixed sex groups and worked in two large groups on open ended themes such as 'conflict'.

The teacher usually started off a lesson with a game such as 'sharks', which was often followed by relaxation exercises and 'imaginative mime', i.e. asking pupils to work on their own and, without talking, to imagine that they were in various places, e.g. on the beach, at home. Lessons then proceeded with groups or pairs working on some ideas and then either demonstrating them or joining in a class activity. Occasionally the teacher played roles during a class session. It is interesting to note that the topics she chose were often of social significance and were of immediate concern to the pupils.

I have decided to give examples of work in the second and third terms to indicate the kinds of development that took place as a result of child directed improvisations. I have given a transcription of a lesson in the second term so that an idea can be given of the way in which the teacher introduces an idea and how the children actually develop it. The example given of the third term's work is a mixture of description and transcription.

Examples of child centred group improvisations

TERM TWO – IMPROVISATIONS ROUND PARENT AND TEENAGER PROBLEMS

TEACHER What were we doing last week? I know some people were away. I left you to get on with some work and you were in groups of about three or four. Remember we started looking at problems of people of your own age or perhaps a bit older and your parents within *ordinary* situations like buying shoes when, um, your mum wants to buy one thing and you want another, and then you discussed favouritism – when one brother always seems to get his own way – or whatever it was. What was it you illustrated?

EMMA Who was going to watch the television.

TEACHER And what else?

CHRIS About going out an' all that.

TEACHER What we discussed was the kind of simpler problems but we also said that there were more serious problems – the kind that crop up in certain families and because certain things had happened. Now let's see if each group could make a play about one of these problems. I can't remember which the groups were, but I know that the group over there were working on something quite interesting ... One or two people haven't really managed to organise themselves. You've tried perhaps to jump too soon. ... Get into your groups and talk about what the problem is and how you're going to illustrate it. You are going to show a group of people a play, and we hope what we see is going to be interesting, but we hope also that what we are going to see is perhaps going to show us something that is truthful about certain families, certain people. You know, what about welfare – whose decision is it if a child who's being neglected is taken away from the home? So any problem you like. Someone else mentioned the problem of teenagers getting involved with drugs . . .

In case people are stuck for ideas, can we name some of the things that some of you think are some of the *bigger* problems?

ADRIANA Joining in a Hell's Angel gang that your mother doesn't approve of.

SUE If you have a row with your mother and you know what really upsets her and then you go out and do your stupid stuff and then you come back and say 'Guess what I did, I beat up this old man' – like you're trying to get your own back. You don't like it much . . .

TEACHER Ah, so you think that the cause of a lot of trouble is being spiteful to one another?

TIM Money.

TEACHER Money? In what way?

TIM Pocket money.

TEACHER What about the trouble that mum and dad have to face up to the fact that their child has been in trouble with the law, caught stealing? . . . How do parents react?

In each case, pick a particular problem and think, how are we going to dramatise it? . . . (*They get into groups.*)

The group described spent half of the lesson discussing what to do and who to be. First they tried the theme of belonging to a gang. After about five minutes they decided the 'story was too weak' and started on a second situation – the school scene – parts of which are transcripted below. It was about a child who stole some money from a cloakroom. He was caught and his parents told.

ADAM You have a bag or something and you just pop it in and walk out.

ARTHUR Are you going to do it?

TIM Yes. O.K.

ADAM Let's start. (*They practise about three times.*)

ARTHUR Ring, ring. (*Simulates the sound of a phone.*)

CHRIS (*Sitting in a chair in his shirt sleeves, sipping tea and watching the television*) Hello.

ARTHUR Stop. Stop. We have to work out a reason.

ADAM O.K. He hasn't got any pocket money and everyone else in his class has, so . . .

ARTHUR O.K.

ADAM (*To Tim*) So what's your name then?

TIM Chris Brady.

ADAM As a head, my name's Dobson.

CHRIS Right. So they catch him with four quid on him and they get him in. (*They act it out. Chris pretends to be a teacher, catches Tim in the cloakroom and drags him into the office.*)

ADAM You silly nit. Knock first.

CHRIS Oh, sorry. (*Does it again.*)

ADAM Ring, ring.

ARTHUR Father. Hello.

ADAM This is Dobson here. It's about your son. He's stolen four pounds from the cloakroom.

ARTHUR My son? I don't believe it.

ADAM Perhaps you could come over.

ARTHUR Certainly. (*Bursts into the room and shouts at Tim.*) Well, what have you got to say? (*Tim is speechless.*)

ADAM Well, it seemed that he didn't show up for class according to Mr Clark, the history teacher, so he went to look for him. Keep your head up boy. Stand straight. Sit down please.

ARTHUR What have you got to say? (*Lunges towards Tim.*)

ADAM Sit down. Sit down.

ARTHUR Just you wait till you get home.

ADAM Now. What to do with you. What have you got to say?

TIM Please Sir, I never have no money, an' I want to go to the football with my friends and he never gives me none.

ADAM Two weeks suspension off. And a good caning at home.

TIM Thank you, Sir. Thank you, Sir.

ADAM Give your son some pocket money and he won't do this again.

ARTHUR What! Are you telling me what to do with my son? . . . Well, all right, I suppose I could. Come on, son, let's go.

This short extract shows that the boys were beginning to impose some form of shape on their scene. They worked out reasons as to why the boy behaved as he did and brought the scene to a conclusion, whereas in the first term they were still working out scenes sequentially. As a group they still worked well together and the way they portrayed the characters physically showed more detail and more response to each other. For instance, the son showed a mixture of fear and hostility towards his father, whereas in term one he would simply have run away from his father.

When the teacher asked the class to discuss the scene, they talked in terms of performance, e.g. 'He was underacting like. He just stood there', whereas the teacher was interested in discussing the issues which caused conflict between father and son.

TERM THREE – LIBERATION

In this term the groups were enlarged to nine and the teacher gave them an open ended theme of 'conflict'. She allowed them to work on their own for most of the time and they spent a number of lessons working on their scenes. One group chose the theme of a small village taken over by Roman soldiers. The group I observed in detail decided to do something on women's liberation. They started with a discussion amongst themselves about the equality of the sexes.

ADAM Females can't do what men can like run the country and make things and . . .

EMMA What rubbish. You don't know anything about anything. Women are members of Parliament.

ADRIANA And who brings you up and tells you what to do?

ARTHUR Well, I think they're the same 'cause we can all do the same things.

CHRIS (*Snickers.*)

JOSIE Shut up. Yeah, I agree. We can do as well as you.

EMMA Then what's the trouble then?

ARTHUR Well, I think they're the same 'cause we can all do the same.

During the work out sessions, it was interesting to note that most of the organising was done by three children. Although the others chipped in, gave ideas and joined in the activities, they generally did what the three leaders wanted. Much more discussion than usual preceded the action and eventually the group decided that the issue at stake was that two groups wanted power to order the other group around. The scene that eventually emerged during the work out phase was one where the boys sat round an imaginary board table watching the girls doing cleaning work in a factory. The girls then complained about the working conditions and one girl suggested they complain to the men.

ADRIANA Look here, we want a meeting.
ADAM A meeting? The ladies want a meeting. You'll have your meeting and then you'll be sacked. You hear. Sacked.
OTHER BOYS Outrageous. Hear, hear.
EMMA Well, we're complaining about our conditions, working hour after hour in these filthy rooms.
JOSIE No tea breaks.
ADRIANA An' you haven't paid us for, um, for um . . .
EMMA Four months.
ARTHUR Go away.

The girls went into a huddle and started muttering 'demonstrate, demonstrate'. They then did a kind of war dance round the men chanting 'liberation, liberation'. The boys all turned their backs. The girls climbed on to the table and pushed the boys off.

The next scene comprised the boys doing the manual work with the girls in charge. The same attempts at discussion and demonstration were made until the boys were standing on the table with the girls.

ANGELA Wait, wait. I've an idea. Can't we do it together? (*Everyone talked at once.*)
ARTHUR Let's work together.
(They leapt off the table and, chanting 'liberation', all started scrubbing. After a while they started scrubbing in slow motion, muttering about how unpleasant it was.)
ADAM I've got a brilliant idea. Let's buy robots who can do the work so that we don't do nothing. (*Cheering from everybody. They all got back on to the table and danced together. End.*)

COMMENTS

A number of different things emerged in this term. The first was that groups were larger and of mixed sexes. Within the groups, not all members participated equally – about three or four did most of the work although all pupils took part. Pupils who had remained outside groups before were absorbed into the groups. The groups were more interested in the issues at stake than in qualities of performance. During discussions there were often lively exchanges about differences of opinion. In spite of change of emphasis, performance had improved. Situations were clearly portrayed, easy to see and easy to hear. This seemed to correspond with an improvement in form which in turn seemed to be a result of the pupils having clearer ideas about the issues involved and how to execute them. This might have been due to increased cooperation between members and length of experience. It is interesting that the more sophisticated the portrayal (e.g. the scene quoted above) the more some form of symbolism seemed to occur to express ideas, e.g. turning of backs, use of the level of the table to denote power. It is possible that symbolism occurs only when a group has reached a certain level of conceptualisation, where complex ideas need to be expressed in simple and clearly understood ways.

The general uses of child centred group improvisations

In child centred group improvisations, the responsibility for producing end products lies with the children. Not only do they have to negotiate with each other the choices they wish to make about the scene created, but they have to use their own resources for ideas. This gives children an opportunity to work at their own levels and to explore aspects of relevance to them personally. It is a useful way of encouraging children to formulate, try out, order and express their ideas. Because these ideas are often about people, the situations people find themselves in, or fantasies about various things e.g. ghosts, the dramatic form is a useful means of exploration. Teachers may get bored when children go over and over the same situation, e.g. 'The haunted house', without realising anything. Perhaps this is the children's way of exploring issues important to them at that time. The problem for the teacher is to know how to help children to stretch themselves, and to know what stage of development the children have reached.

In looking at the development of group improvisation of three classes over a year, the results seemed to indicate that progress occurred along the lines of development described in this case study – i.e. improvisations progressed from pupils arguing about who was going to be what character, to working out the situations by trial and error, to conceptualising the situation before enacting it, to discussions about authenticity of characters. Clarity of gesture, characterisation and detail improved as the children became more certain about what they were doing. This meant that the performances of the scenes created also gained in clarity, and there was less vagueness and muddle. It seemed that the more interested they were in the content of their work and in how the characters related to that, the better their performances were, even though they had no acting and voice exercises to improve the quality of performance. These are probably only necessary if the work that children have created is going to be taken a stage further and polished for more public performance. Communication to a larger audience, where children have to be heard and seen over a greater distance, then becomes a problem. Usually, however, with small group improvisations, groups show their work, if at all, to the rest of the class in more intimate conditions.

Child centred group improvisation is therefore useful for three main reasons: 1 It gives children the opportunity of trying out ideas they are personally interested in, ordering them and expressing them in dramatic form. 2 Because of this it gives children the experience of what it is like to create an art form and to make effective personal statements. 3 Every child in the group has responsibility for making it work. It is therefore a valuable form of social education where children have to cooperate and work creatively.

7 The use of drama as a service subject

The use of drama as a service subject in a primary school

The primary school in which the drama described in this chapter took place is in an urban area. The children come from predominantly working class homes. There is, however, a fair spread of ability even though there is a high proportion of immigrants. The school is a red brick building with classrooms leading off a hall. Teachers are allowed the use of the hall generally once a week. Otherwise children work with their teacher in the classroom or outside for sports.

The class studied is of thirty ten year olds. It spans the ability range. The teacher is interested in general problems of literacy as well as wanting to encourage children to be able to discuss issues and express their feelings fluently and thoughtfully. In addition to the type of work about to be described, this teacher also teaches other forms of drama – a lot of pure movement, small group work and whole group work, often exploring a story of historical or social significance. Discussion plays a large part in her teaching and she expects children to give adequate reasons for their opinions.

I have chosen her work to illustrate how a subject can be taught through drama because in primary schools teachers have a great deal of scope to use drama as part of their general work with children.

Because this type of drama concentrates on finding out more about particular subjects, it would be of little use to describe the development of the work over a long period of time. Rather, I shall concentrate on one lesson to show how drama can be used to complement what children have learnt in other ways.

Example of using drama as a method to explore a topic

The teacher wanted the children to find out about mining and the problems involved in it. She used the miners' strike of 1972 as a starting point, and explored the subject in a variety of ways. She wanted to give children an idea of how mining developed in technical and social terms and, for instance, what conditions were like in the past.

BACKGROUND MATERIAL TO THE LESSON

A number of books and 'Jackdaws' served as source material for the history of mining. The children were shown pictures of poverty and disease; they reacted strongly to these, and especially to those of children and women working in the mines. A number of geography books showed the children where mines were located and how coal was formed and mined; topic books, newspaper cuttings and films were made available for children to get an idea of the contemporary scene. Children made personal folders about the subject and painted pictures illustrating either mining technology or conditions in the mines. Discussions were held about the amount of pay miners ought to get; according to the teacher, the general opinion was that they ought to be well paid. The teacher hoped that through drama the pupils could explore what it felt like to be a miner or the family of a miner under threat of a mining accident.

THE DRAMA LESSON

This began with free movement which was gradually restricted so that children were moving as if they were in cramped passages, often in difficult conditions. They were then expected to imagine they were down a mine, doing various physical tasks like cutting the face, carrying the coal or investigating dangerous places.

A discussion then took place concerning the kinds of accidents that could occur in mines, and the teacher asked them what kind of accident they would like to explore in drama. They suggested a flood and wanted some members to be warned about the flood before others, so that they could go for help. It was agreed that a member of a group nearest the surface of the mine would begin the warning and that this would be passed down to the other groups. The teacher asked members of the class to decide individually whether they were going to be injured or not.

Small groups set to work. When the signal came everyone reacted as though they had been struck violently. The teacher stopped the action to remind them that if the accident was a flood caused by a rock fall, they would react differently.

The signal was given again and the pupils reacted with better effect. The children imagined the scene in more detail – rocks fell on some, some escaped, others experienced a series of difficulties, climbing on ledges and crawling through tunnels. Rescuers arrived with various instruments and rescue devices. The teacher said that the children were very concerned about the state of the injured and took care to hurt them as little as possible. She felt that this was a direct result of doing a lot of practice in various trust exercises in movement, e.g. lifting and balancing.

In addition to the children dramatising a disaster scene in the mines, the teacher wanted to explore what it was like to have a miner as a relative. The class was divided into families. One member of each family worked down a mine. The families were told of an accident in the mine and hurried to the mine to wait for survivors to emerge. The tension was realistic and members of families discussed what they would do if their relative was killed or injured. They were all relieved when they found that there were no deaths.

The teacher then asked them if they had imagined what it might be like to wait like that and what would happen to the family if their breadwinner died. She commented on how realistic their answers had been as a result of the improvisation. They were then asked to write down their experiences. The amount of detail in the written work revealed that they had memorised some of the technology in the mines in their drama work. They were able to visualise what it might have been like to be down the mines and their descriptions of how they felt in situations of danger were convincing. Descriptions generally were vivid and full of human content without neglecting the more factual sides of mining as well. The teacher pointed out that the quality of work had been achieved through working in a variety of ways and that a great deal of back up work had gone on before exploration in drama had taken place.

Looking at disasters was one aspect of mining. The teacher also wanted the children to have an idea of administrative relations in mining. Taking the strike as a focal point, she thought it would be relevant to set up a mock television interview to look at the relationships between union men, managers and politicians.

A conflict situation was set up between picketers and workers or drivers trying to break through the groups. A few children acted as reporters who interviewed all parties. Those who didn't strike gave reasons such as they felt they earned enough money or that they had large families and could not afford to strike. Strikers were then interviewed with the employers. The teacher felt that this was a worthwhile experience for the interviewer because he had to maintain order in a tricky situation. After the interviews, discussions followed in which all parties' points of view were taken into account. The teacher commented that some of them had been so involved in their characters that they found it difficult to argue objectively. On the whole, because of their previous drama lesson, they felt more sympathy for the miners because of the dangers they faced.

The children were so enthusiastic about their work that they wanted to show it to other children. They did this during assembly with a display of their paintings, readings from their prose and poetry, and a performance of clashes between pickets and non-miners, followed by television interviews. At the end of the session they asked the audience to make their own decisions regarding the miners' pay.

COMMENTS

This description of how a teacher explored mining is a good example of how a contemporary issue can be explored through an integrated approach using history, geography, science, art, writing, and drama. It means that children can see the subject from a variety of viewpoints.

The teacher was able to gauge how much they had learnt through setting them written work which was structured in such a way that she could find out if they had assimilated the facts involved and also whether they understood what the issues were.

These children experienced what it might have been like to have been in a mining disaster. They also gained some idea of the kinds of problems encountered when industrial negotiations take place.

General methods of using drama as a service subject

It is hoped that this case study has indicated how drama can be used in learning about a topic. Enacting a situation means that the subject can be understood at a different level. Children are given the opportunity of actively imagining what it might be like to be in certain situations. They are made physically and mentally to react to being in situations, either as themselves, or in roles. This gives the subject a more vivid significance and makes it more personally relevant to each child. Because it can be a vivid and sometimes emotional experience, as seen in the exploration of a mining disaster, this approach can have dangers. Children might remember dramatic episodes which may distort their understanding of the whole. In this particular case, for instance, the teacher may have presented her material in such a way that the miners were favoured to the detriment of the management. These considerations should not however detract from the great contribution that drama can make to the understanding of a particular theme.

8 Drama as training for the theatre: an example of a 'theatre arts' course

General picture of the school

The last case study takes place in an all girls comprehensive school of 1,100 pupils. The school is in an urban working class area with a large Greek Cypriot and West Indian community. It has an eight form entry. Some subjects are unstreamed and integrated subjects are taught in the first two years. Many of the girls leave before the sixth form because they have no respect for education. The school attempts to give them an all round education, i.e. the opportunity to experience a number of subjects. The most popular subject is typewriting.

The school is relatively modern and the buildings spread over a large area of ground so that children have to walk a distance to go from one subject to another.

The school is very aware of the community and attempts to have links with them through active P.T.A.s, and performances. The girls are active in the local Task Force and spend afternoons looking after old people. Every Christmas the girls put on a Christmas show for the old age pensioners in the area.

At the time the study was taking place, the school had a drama department. This consisted of a head of department, three full time specialists – one of whom spent a lot of time teaching social studies, and one part time teacher who specialised in speech. Drama was compulsory in the first three years. The first two years had drama for a double period and the third year had drama for a single period. There was a drama optional C.S.E. course for fourth and fifth year pupils. In the sixth form a term of drama is offered as part of a liberal studies course.

The pupils

Because a C.S.E. course is being looked at, the girls concerned were studied over a period of two years. They were aged fifteen when the course started. Every student had had three years of educational drama previous to starting the course and most of them were enthusiastic because they had chosen the course as an option. There were twenty pupils to start with but the numbers dropped as pupils left the school. Two members were regular truants and seldom attended. The ability range was fairly mixed ranging from three girls in the top ability range to two girls who could hardly read.

The drama room

Drama mainly took place in a utility built drama room. This room was also used as a classroom which meant that tables had to be pushed back. It was sometimes also used as a dining room because it was near a kitchen. Because of this it was not possible to store any useful props etc.

The hall which adjoined the room was also occasionally used but not often because of interruptions when classes passed through going from one building to another. In spite of this the spaces were adequate and the rooms pleasant to work in, thus creating a useful working atmosphere.

Teacher's attitudes and aims

The teacher had two main problems; how to cope with a class where the range of ability was extremely wide and how to devise a syllabus that would take into account the pupils' previous drama work, much of which included unstructured improvisations, while stretching the girls as much as possible. As the course progressed, it became clear that there were only nine regular attenders; the rest came and went depending on whether they were needed for other activities such as sport, Task Force, career interviews etc. This meant that the course had to be flexible enough to cope with fluctuating numbers, including a number of girls who had not enrolled on the course but turned up every now and then.

C.S.E. Mode III: Theatre Arts course

It was hoped that the girls would extend their normal drama work and acting abilities. Their own work would culminate in an improvised play that had been polished for performance. This would give them a chance to see what it is like to devise, work out and perform a play. They would also be required to put on a performance of a scripted play at the end of the course either as actresses or from the stage management side. They should leave with a knowledge of how to work backstage as well as how to act.

In addition to this practical side, which also included acting, movement and speech exercises, the activity of drama was put into a cultural context. Pupils were given some idea of various aspects of the history of the theatre, read a number of scripts from various periods, went to a local educational theatre to find out what to do behind the scenes, and paid numerous visits to the professional theatre. Because the teacher felt that the mass media ought to be studied as well, girls found out how television and film programmes were made and visited television studios and television and film museums.

At the end of the course all the girls were expected (a) to participate in final productions where they would be involved as actresses and in stage management – sometimes as directors. At the end of the first year they did their improvised play and at the end of the second year they did extracts from a number of plays; (b) to do some individual research on a theme that each girl would choose. These varied from 'How life in Shakespeare's time affected the theatre', to 'A study of how the sets and costumes of two plays were designed' (for the more practical, costumes were designed and made and models and sets constructed), to 'A criticism of current drama series on B.B.C.1 today'; (c) write an examination concerning the theoretical aspects of the course. They were expected to have some idea of the history of the theatre – the type of social background to certain kinds of plays; the main themes of a certain period; history of costume and set design. Five plays from various periods were studied in some detail and they were expected to know what the play was about and its significance. They were also expected to be able to write about aspects of stage management, e.g. how to write a sound or lighting plot, what sorts of props a certain play might need or the principles of make-up so that they would know how to make up for certain characters.

Examples of work done during the course

HISTORY OF THE THEATRE

These pupils were not academically inclined and had very little background of reading literature or history. Formal script reading of plays would therefore be a waste of time. It was thus decided to try to give the girls a flavour of the period in which the play took place, an idea of the type of subject matter people were concerned with. The teacher gave them the plot and they worked out sections of the play that the teacher thought they could handle. Groups were then asked to work out sections of plays in the light of what they had learnt about the social setting, the costume and stage designs of a particular period and to show it to the other pupils. In this way each group could work in depth on two or three periods and experience plays of other periods as members of an audience. Having to present extracts of work at the end of each term gave the girls a great deal of incentive and the teacher a good idea of whether they had grasped the flavour of an age or had understood a particular script. Where relevant models of costumes and theatres were made they added a visual dimension to the work.

When it was felt that the girls understood the historical background of a play, emphasis was given to understanding the content of the play and groups were asked to devise ways of putting content across so that it was more understandable.

Examples will be given of work done on the Greek, Mediaeval and Shakespearian periods. In all cases a preliminary talk was given about the period and plays concerned. This was presented in the form of handouts with work sheets attached to give the girls reference materials for their examinations. They were shown pictures or diagrams of the theatres and what people looked like. They were given various period dances to do to catch a flavour of what it might have felt like to have performed in that period. A particular play was then discussed and parts of it studied. Groups were formed and then asked which parts of the play they would like to perform. They then decided on the mode of performance.

(a) The Trojan Women The play studied was *The Trojan Women* by Euripides. The girls working on this play wanted to achieve a blend of period setting with a modern flavour so that the relevance of the play's message about war could be seen in contemporary terms. They studied Greek vases in the British Museum to get some idea of the gestures of Greek dancers and they decided to do an extract from the chorus condemning war. This was enacted by dancing and chanting. The choreography, gestures and costumes were based on pictures from the Greek vases they had studied, but the music was done in the idiom of contemporary pop. One girl strummed a guitar while the actors performed and the performance, although very short, was most effective.

(b) Miracle plays: The Story of Noah The group who chose *The Story of Noah* felt that they wanted as authentic a flavour as possible. They created a market scene in which the audience participated and erected a moving platform on which the play appeared. It was done extremely simply, straight from the script; costumes were mediaeval and conventions such as angels appearing at the top of the platform were adhered to.

(c) Othello The girls who tackled *Othello* were intrigued by the plot. They were a group of West Indian girls, half of whom found it difficult to read any script, let alone Shakespeare, fluently. They went through the jealousy scene word for word until they knew it almost

by heart. They then translated the scene into Creole, put the play in a modern gangster setting and produced a very convincing violent interpretation of the play.

These three scenes were performed at the end of a term and were thoroughly enjoyed. It proved that with the help of drama it is possible for non-academic children to learn about things that they otherwise would not enjoy.

Practical work on the history of the theatre was useful because the girls were able to illustrate what they had learnt in dramatic terms. It gave them practice in appearing before audiences. It helped them build up confidence for the time when they had to put on larger scale performances.

WORKING TOWARDS PERFORMANCES

A play was improvised about a murder in which every member had a motive for killing the victim, an old lady. The story was devised by the girls and directed by one of them. Each girl worked on her own character in depth doing characterisation exercises and building up facts about herself, her personality and age etc. The story was arrived at after lengthy argument and discussion because most of the pupils felt that it was unsatisfactory. The problem was that they wanted to give everyone a part of equal importance, but also had to cope with the fact that some of the girls were unreliable attenders. As a result, the play was episodic and had few real points of tension. The characters came over as rather dull although the whole thing ran smoothly. The important lesson learnt by this performance was the difficulty of writing reasonable plays with interesting characters that could sustain interest. The girls were much more appreciative of the quality of scripted plays after this attempt. One girl remarked that it was easy during spontaneous improvisation to catch 'high' moments, but it was not so easy to repeat them and capture the same intensity.

The problem with scripted plays for girls is to find plays with sufficient female roles or where the parts can effectively be played by either sex. The girls were given a range of scripts from different periods to choose from. They were told that it didn't matter whether they did extracts from one play or different scenes from various plays. This particular group split in two. One half wanted to do a scene from *The Caucasian Chalk Circle* where the heroine marries a dying man who wakes up in the middle of the wedding. They liked the humour of the situation and the technical difficulties of staging it. Because there could be many characters in the wedding scene, it gave some girls the opportunity of trying a number of parts. The other girls were fascinated by Pinter and wanted to do a double bill of *The Room* and *The Dumbwaiter*. They liked his use of language and, after a great deal of work, realised the importance of timing, i.e. how to use pauses for effect. The interesting thing was that the girls who found reading difficult quickly memorised their lines and showed by the quality of their expressions that they understood the words they delivered. As there were two groups each girl could help behind the stage to make the other group's scene go smoothly. They all therefore had first hand experience of lighting etc., and were able to appreciate the whole experience of putting on a play.

Not all the pupils had the same talent for acting. Some of them were unable to become imaginatively involved and were therefore more wooden and less convincing than others, no matter what amount of movement training, improvisation or speech training they had had. Because the examination marks gave equal weighting to their projects, performances and examinations, most of the girls had a chance of doing reasonably well as they could concentrate on their best activities. When asked whether they thought they had gained from the course, they said they felt they had been stretched and had learnt a great deal about different aspects of the theatre.

Comments

This course gave the girls an opportunity to see how their previous drama work linked with the outside theatre: by trying to make their own play and produce it, they were able to experience the difficulties professional people have. The practicalities of performing and producing scripted plays enabled them to understand the content of written plays better. It helped them to learn what it is like to appear on stage and put across other people's characters and thoughts, and also what it is like to be responsible for the smooth running of the play behind the stage.

A study of historical aspects of the theatre put their work in a wider context. They gained some knowledge of the background of the theatre and the various ways in which drama can be used to express different kinds of ideas.

This and the other theoretical aspects that girls were expected to study were included in the course for very definite reasons. It was thought that because the girls came from backgrounds in which it was not normal to go to the theatre, let alone be aware of the cultural and historical background to it, a more mentally demanding approach would give them a wider understanding and experience of the world in which they lived. By introducing it in as practical a manner as possible, it was hoped that it would be more palatable to the most anti-academic girls in the course.

The uses of theatre arts courses in drama

Unlike other forms of educational drama which could be said to be of use to most students, the study of theatre arts is useful specifically for pupils who wish to specialise in drama. You can do drama without learning performance skills or knowing anything about the background of the theatre or how plays are put on. Theatre arts courses are therefore quite rightly optional and serve students who have a special interest in the subject.

Most theatre arts courses teach two main things: (i) About the 'theatre' and how it works: how to understand plays better, how plays are put on in a stage management sense, the historical background to the theatre and facets of design – both sets and costumes. (ii) A knowledge about theatre is complemented by practical experience of the theatre – this includes the perfection of acting and performing techniques and how to stage manage a performance. Children who have been through this kind of training are more aware of the work involved in putting on theatrical performances and can therefore appreciate and criticise them on different levels.

9 Summary and conclusion of five case studies

Summary

In this part of the book I have attempted to give examples of some of the main ways in which drama can be used. Five case histories indicating the use of different methods have been given. It is important to note that the examples of work described should be seen in the unique context in which the drama was conducted. They are model lessons but are meant to show how certain teaching methods used in drama can be adapted to the needs of the particular pupils being taught. Examples were given of work by children in a grammar school, a remedial class in a comprehensive school, a mixed ability class, fourth year girls in an all girls comprehensive, and by primary school children. According to a teacher's specific aims and intentions, all these methods could be adapted to suit any of these children.

The first kind of drama described how a particular skill could be used as a basis for drama work. It was shown how grammar school boys could learn to express themselves physically as well as verbally. The teacher began by teaching them formal mime techniques rather than a freer type of movement which they might not have responded to. The general use of other kinds of movement, usually as warm ups to lessons, were also described. These include Laban type movement, where children are taught to use various parts of their body, space, differences in speed etc. This type of movement is frequently practised in conjunction with interpersonal work where trust exercises are done to encourage children to work cooperatively. Movement training of these types are intended to give children physical confidence, coordination and control, and a movement vocabulary in which to express themselves. An additional type of movement was described where children are asked to imagine they are in certain physical conditions and to act as if they have certain objects around them. This is similar to formal mime except that there are no formal gestures or procedures to learn. In both cases children are taught to be more perceptive about the space and objects around them, and this enhanced perception makes the task of creating an imaginary environment a great deal easier for many of them.

The second method described was teacher directed drama in which the teacher role played. For the particular children described (remedial), the method was used as a secure framework in which children could begin to be imaginatively involved in a dramatic activity and begin to work with their peers without conflict. It was also suggested that the method could be used to teach subjects like history where the teacher could control the feeding in of the material and direct the progress of the lesson to make a particular scene as factually realistic as possible. Another way in which role play by the teacher could be used is where the class is involved in making up a whole group play, but where the story line is channelled by the teacher so that certain general topics are explored through the story (e.g. the topic of keeping public secrets).

The difference between teacher directed drama and child centred drama is that in the latter, the responsibility for an end product lies with the children concerned. The case study described here shows how a group of boys and girls were able to work together to investigate a topic which particularly interested them at that time – the 'liberation' question, in their case both of men and women. It was suggested that this method can have social, cognitive and artistic uses. Children have to work together as a group to produce an end product. They have to agree among themselves about what they are going to do and what criteria for success they feel they should have. Making up a group play means that after they have been given an initial stimulus they have to use their own resources to think up ideas, order them into some kind of shape, and finally express those ideas in a communicable form. This involves a combination of cognitive, affective and artistic activities. They have to represent their feelings about certain topics through the dramatic form.

The teacher's problem is how to develop this form of drama. It can move from children arriving at situations by trial and error to pre-planned scenes about well thought out ideas; from the portrayal of stereotyped roles to characterisations of people who have personalities, motives and feelings for other people. Although my own research seems to indicate that there is a progression, more research needs to be done if this is to be substantiated.

The next method described does not necessarily require much initiative from the children. Drama can be used very simply as a teaching method to reinforce children's understanding of a subject. I have suggested that this can be done through teacher directed role playing. I chose an example of work in a primary school and showed how a topic such as mining could be enriched by the use of drama. This kind of work is particularly relevant to primary schools because there the teacher can decide when to use drama without the kind of constraints that most secondary schools have about rigid timetabling. This method does not need training in acting skills as it is merely intended to give children a chance to realise what certain situations might have been like. It gives pupils experience of how they, as individuals, might have reacted in similar circumstances, or, if they play roles, how another kind of person might react.

The final kind of drama mentioned treats it as both a subject and a method. It is studied by pupils who are interested in how the finished art form is written, performed and produced professionally. It is taken by pupils, usually in the fourth and fifth years, as an examination subject and is of benefit to those who wish to specialise as drama professionals after school or those who are interested in the theatre or wish to act in an amateur capacity. Drama as a 'theatre art' is optional and studied by a few interested pupils whereas other forms of educational drama could be applied to all pupils.

Similarities and differences found in the methods described

The five case studies indicated different ways in which drama can be used in education. These differences, however, are differences in degree rather than in kind. In Part I the central aims and concepts found in drama were described. In the course of conversations with the five teachers involved in these case histories, it became clear that many of these aims were common to the work of all teachers although they differed in emphasis.

I now intend to look at some of the similarities and differences found in the types of drama described, so that the reader can draw a more general picture of the practice of the subject.

THE USE OF IMAGINATION AND CREATIVITY

In all cases, children were expected to suspend belief, to pretend that they were in 'as if' situations, usually as different characters from themselves. This meant that they had to extend their perceptions and allow for the possibility of happenings that were not directly related to their present circumstances. These include, for instance, opening an imaginary door, going on an imagined journey, pretending to be in a factory, being down a mine or acting from a script. The more imaginative the child, the more his portrayals of imagined scenes are detailed and approximate to reality. The child who learns to perceive and recall people and situations in more detail and more accurately will probably have an increased capacity for recall and understanding.

In drama, imagination is not enough. Once they have imagined 'as if' situations and characters, children have to act on those assumptions – they have to react and interact. Situations and characters become developed and elaborated as the action proceeds. This means that children have to create them in order for the drama to develop. The scope for creativity depends on a number of factors: i.e., in teacher directed drama, a child in an imagined journey can invent a slight accident, e.g. spill a glass of beer, but is limited to working within the structure that the teacher has directed for him. His character has to react within a clearly defined setting and time. This does not give him a great deal of scope to elaborate in depth the character he is playing. The experience can still be valuable to the child, however, if he learns to understand the nature of the particular activity enacted. In child directed drama, on the other hand, the child has to be as creative as possible, not only in inventing a situation and a story line, but also in creating characters and the relationships between characters in such a way that the drama is plausible. In addition to inventing characters and small situations, children working like this have to create an end product. This means that they have to be creative in small as well as in overall contexts.

FORMS OF EXPRESSION

In drama, the body and voice are used as the media to express ideas, via characterisation and role play. The teacher can assess how imaginative or inventive a child is by seeing and hearing what he does. In the first case history, the form of expression was almost exclusively physical. In all the others it was verbal as well as physical. In some cases children expressed ideas that they had thought up and enacted. In other cases children expressed their reactions as characters within tightly structured situations. Children often gain great satisfaction from expressing ideas and feelings in verbal and physical form. The quality of their performance is sometimes thought to be secondary to the pleasure they derive from the experience itself. When the drama acted is to be communicated, however, more emphasis is given to formal skills. Actions then take on the quality of performance and more attention is focused on the way that people present themselves on the stage. To some extent, child centred improvisations, when they are shown, concentrate on communication. The main form of training for performance comes in theatre arts courses when children have to act in finished productions for outside audiences. Children also learn about performance when they are putting on school plays or other productions for the school.

THE USE OF SKILLS IN DRAMA

All the teachers used some form of warm up in the course of their teaching. They all felt that movement training was useful for children because it relaxed them, gave them confidence and supplied them with ideas for a range of expression that they otherwise would not have. One teacher used hardly any movement, not because he did not want to, but because he had no space available. All forms of movement were used depending on whether teachers wanted to encourage control, experimentation, cooperation between pupils or imaginative involvement.

Some teachers used games to start off lessons. They ranged from purely physical games like 'sharks', where the teacher called out a number of instructions to which children had to react physically and quickly, to verbal games where children had to remember what had been said before and build a story on it. These games were often an easy way to get children to work together and created an atmosphere of enjoyment. Often they were used to encourage physical and verbal dexterity.

In a few cases speech exercises were used to help children express themselves in more ways than they were accustomed to. A typical exercise was to ask children to pretend they were communicating in a foreign language and to make themselves understood just by the use of intonation and volume. This was fun and encouraged pupils to use the full range of their voices. Articulation and other exercises were used for children in theatre training when they had difficulty in projecting their voices. I had the distinct impression, however, that formal speech training was a thing of the past.

Skills of all sorts were generally used to get children in a good working frame of mind and to enable them to express themselves more freely and effectively.

The social nature of drama

Drama by its nature is concerned with social interaction. It is involved with interaction on a make believe and also on a real level. Children learn to work as a group. The dramatic activity cannot take place effectively if children do not agree to work cooperatively. Giving and accepting ideas, acting on your own and others' ideas, working together to make sense of what you are doing, all of these are part of the social aspect of drama. It can, depending on the kind of drama taught, encourage children to learn to work together in a creative environment, solve problems creatively and work out corporate ways of expressing their own feelings and ideas.

Factors influencing the kind of drama taught

There are certain factors which seem particularly to influence what happens in any drama lesson. These include

1 the general aims of the lesson
2 the amount of direction in the lesson
3 the treatment of subject matter
4 the size of the groups participating
5 the main kinds of dramatic activities in the lesson, e.g. whether role play or mime are emphasised
6 how the lesson is concluded: whether the lesson is geared towards an end product, e.g. a performance, or not, or whether it ends in discussion.

1 THE GENERAL AIMS OF THE LESSON

If a teacher wishes to teach children miming techniques he is going to have different aims from the teacher who wishes to explore a particular aspect of history through drama. Each teacher's intentions regarding the particular children he is teaching will differ. Even though many teachers will not be clear about what they want to do and will often improvise during a lesson, they do encourage development along definite lines (for example, towards performance). It is therefore the teacher's attitudes towards his work and his own interests within the subject that will determine his choice of the activities in the lesson. In this respect drama differs from the teaching of other subjects where there exists a specific body of knowledge to be acquired, and it reinforces the point made before that there is no set way of teaching drama.

2 THE AMOUNT OF DIRECTION IN THE LESSON

Some drama lessons are more teacher directed than others. This depends on whether the teacher wishes children to perfect particular skills, or to work within a tight framework. Heavily directed drama lessons can be useful in giving children security or for teaching them about a topic by controlling the input of facts and ideas and the direction of the lesson as a whole. Used in this way it could be a valuable teaching method. Emphasis is placed on the value of children experiencing what it might be like to be in the kinds of situations set up by the teacher; by acting it out, they may be better able to understand certain facets of the subject they are studying. Very heavily directed drama helps the child to become imaginatively involved. It does not, however, allow him to explore his own ideas at his own level and pace, nor to create the actual situations being acted. Neither does it give him much chance to study a character in depth. This type of directed drama is therefore usually connected with role play, where children are given parts that have a specific function: for example, children play the roles of miners down a mine rather than exploring the unique position of an individual personality and the details of his personal life.

When children are responsible for creating and shaping their own work, there is more scope for creativity. This is useful as it teaches them to handle their ideas and to express them through dramatic form. It poses a problem for the teacher, however: how best can he improve the quality of the children's work, which can often be pedestrian and incompletely conceived and performed?

We have described one form of teacher directed drama where the teacher carefully structured a travel scene and directed the main activities, and another form of drama where children were given a free hand. Both these examples indicate extremes on a continuum. However, many teachers use a mixture of both forms of drama depending on what they want to achieve. For instance, the teacher demonstrating mime techniques heavily directed the boys until they had gained competence in mime. He then expected them to use their own initiatives in deciding how to use those techniques creatively.

3 THE TREATMENT OF SUBJECT MATTER

Whether a lesson is directed by the teacher or not sometimes depends on the state of development of the pupils. More often, however, it depends on the teacher's choice of theme. The teacher who wishes children to practise interview situations for work is not going to give children an entirely free hand in how they spend the rest of the lesson. The teacher who wants children to explore the process of creating plays might give them a stimulus to work from, but will not mind how they take it up.

4 THE SIZE OF THE GROUPS PARTICIPATING

Often the way a subject is treated will determine the social structure of the lesson. If, for instance, a teacher wishes to do a simulation of a committee in the United Nations, he is more likely to use the whole class. If, on the other hand, he wants the children to explore family situations in their own terms, he will ask small groups to work on the problem. By and large the size of the groups tends to control the amount and type of participation each individual child can have. For instance, if a teacher directs a class's activities the individual can participate in the action and might in a small way be inventive. In large groups where the activity is child directed there are organisation problems: according to teachers who work in this way, a few members of the group tend to be most active and the rest are passive. In small groups, e.g. about five or six, each individual has a chance to contribute to whatever scene is being created but less than that number means that the number of potential ideas is not so large.

5 THE KINDS OF DRAMATIC ACTIVITIES TAKING PLACE

Lessons differ according to the type of activity taking place. For instance, a drama lesson based on mime is unlikely to improve speech, and an imagined court case which consists of arguments for and against a case is unlikely to improve formal mime. Most drama teachers use speech and movement in their work but the quality of the acting will differ depending on what is being explored. It can be free, spontaneous play based on drama, carefully rehearsed performances, depth work on characters or role play in which types rather than individuals are focused upon. The type of activity chosen will not only develop particular skills, but will also determine how superficial or detailed an exploration of a character or situation may be. Improvisations on characters in a scripted play will give more depth to the characters than merely reading a script.

6 HOW THE LESSON IS CONCLUDED

Because there are no simple, clearly defined criteria for judging work in drama, the main way that children will know whether the lesson has succeeded or not, apart from their own evaluations, will be in the way that the teacher discusses or remarks on the work at the end of the lesson. For instance, in a lesson where a teacher is looking at the miners' claims to strike and exploring the issues through drama, it is essential to see whether the children are able to apply their experiences to the issues involved. The drama therefore leads up to a discussion. In a lesson where the whole class is involved in play making, discussion may help the teacher find out what the class thought of the activity and whether they attached any meaning to it.

Often in small group work children are working towards definite end products which will be shown to the rest of the class. They will therefore be under more pressure than in teacher directed work to produce something, usually in a limited period of time. Their work is then judged by the teacher and often by the other pupils, either in terms of the quality of the performance or whether they have effectively said what they want to in ways which satisfy both them and the audience.

A lesson based on working towards a more public performance will have more of a sense of urgency and occasion than other forms of drama. Each lesson will end with comments about how performance can be improved so that the content of the play can come across better.

Lessons will differ depending on whether specific goals are being worked towards or not and the kind of discussion or comment at the end of the lesson will often give pupils cues for what to do next time. They are therefore important.

Examples of work have been given to point out some of the ways in which drama can be taught and what their educational functions could be. Generalisations have been drawn from observations of lessons as to what are the main variables determining differences in drama lessons. These have included aspects like the amount and type of teacher direction and how content is handled. By giving examples of actual work done, I hope that, for the sceptical, a case has been made for the inclusion of drama in the timetables of schools.

It is interesting to note that the organisation of drama in the case study schools reflects the state of drama as portrayed in the survey at the beginning of the book. The two schools in which there were separate drama departments with more than one drama specialist were large comprehensive schools in working class areas. In the comprehensive school where there was a social mix, there was one teacher who had special responsibility for drama within the English department; most of the teachers in that school who taught drama were non-specialists. In the grammar school, one teacher taught drama as part of his English programme because he had a special interest in the subject and had therefore taken a course in it. The primary teacher who taught drama in her school was a general primary teacher who had taken additional training.

Where drama was not fully established, i.e. in the socially mixed comprehensive, the grammar school and the primary school, there was growing interest in the subject. For instance, in the comprehensive the teacher was going to be given a higher graded post and a new studio was being built. In both the primary and grammar schools, interest was coming from other teachers who were prepared to try and teach drama.

This interest reflects a current trend, for more specialist drama teachers are being appointed in schools, more facilities are being built and more children are having drama as a subject on their timetable. In the early seventies, drama was given the status of a scarcity subject – i.e. there was more demand than there were drama teachers.

Counter to this trend are the problems that the economic crisis is bringing. General cutbacks in school staff affect drama teachers as much as other teachers. Because of the reorganisation of teacher training, some drama courses have been discontinued, some new ones have not yet been accepted, and it seems that the number of places for teachers wanting to study drama will drop rather than increase. Cutbacks in both the teaching staff and the advisory service mean that people are having to justify their positions on an unprecedented scale.

These two conflicting elements in drama teaching might explain why the trend in drama circles today seems to be a move away from mainly arguing about controversial issues to discussing the educational value of drama teaching in general. In Part III I intend to go into some of the issues which people now think are important in the development of the subject. These trends will probably influence the way the subject develops in the future.

PART III

Present trends and future developments

Introduction

This book began with a description of the state of drama in schools. It continued with a broad outline of central aims and concepts basic to drama teaching. Linked to this was a discussion about what some of the controversial areas in drama teaching have been. It was suggested that some of the arguments for and against certain drama methods were based on false assumptions about what teachers were trying to achieve through the various methods. Illustrations of five different ways of teaching drama were then given with comments concerning the general uses of each teaching method. Current practice has indicated that there seems to be no set way of teaching drama and that although there are some similarities in skills taught, what the drama teacher does in the class depends on his particular interests and what he feels the state of development of his class to be at a particular time. Drama could therefore be said to be a flexible subject or method which incorporates a variety of approaches and activities. It is this flexibility that is the basis for much confusion regarding the intrinsic value of drama and its justification on the timetable.

In this section I intend to move away from detailed case studies and to consider the general development of drama in the future. At present, the subject seems to be undergoing a series of important changes, both because of pressures from its exponents and because of external factors, including general curriculum change in schools.

In the field a number of people seem to be moving away from

vague feelings that drama is a good thing, to a desire to give a detailed and explicit account of what they are doing. They are becoming more concerned about the quality of their work. This means that some teachers are not just letting children 'get on with it' but are formulating judgements and criteria about how they want children's work to develop. Within some drama circles, therefore, there is a move towards some form of evaluation.

I have already mentioned external factors which are bringing pressures on the drama world to indicate as substantially as possible the sorts of things drama teaching could achieve, i.e. a general move to expand the teaching of drama in schools and the fact that drama specialists are having to defend the maintenance of their subject in the face of economic cutbacks. Drama specialists are being asked to show that drama works, and, in addition, to give people a clear idea of the theoretical basis upon which the teaching of drama is based. At present there is no theoretical overview justifying drama teaching in general as most of the written material is by drama teachers with particular interests.

It is therefore not surprising that the main issues currently being discussed at conferences and meetings have to do with questions of evaluation and the need for a conceptual framework which will articulate those aims and concepts thought by most teachers to form the basis of drama teaching.

I therefore intend to indicate some of the current thinking about evaluation and, linked with evaluation, the question of examinations in drama. As will be shown, there is no general agreement about the subject. For those who believe in drama, there is a great deal of thinking to be done on effective ways of evaluating drama teaching.

It could be argued that evaluation cannot effectively take place unless teachers are clear about their intentions. That could only happen within the context of a theoretical framework which gives adequate grounds and criteria for the teaching of the subject. I would therefore suggest that a rationale for drama teaching needs to be devised before attempts are made to evaluate various dramatic activities. In discussing the need for a theoretical framework, I shall argue that two aspects be taken into account: (i) that the distinctive contribution that drama teaching can make should be studied if claims are to be made that drama can teach things that other subjects cannot; (ii) that the framework should be flexible enough to incorporate a number of approaches and activities.

If a variety of approaches to drama are possible, there might be a number of ways in which it could be timetabled. I shall therefore argue that there is a need for drama teachers to look at the problems of organisation, to see how drama can fit into the timetable, and, more important, to make policy decisions about the amount of time required if children are to be given the maximum opportunity to develop in drama.

Finally, in addition to those issues being currently discussed, I shall finish the book with a few personal recommendations concerning ways in which knowledge of the subject could be improved.

10 Present trends

As with any subject there are always teaching methods that are currently in fashion. In drama, since the subject became popular, there seems to have been a move away from formal speech and drama, where 'performance' was thought important, to child centred group drama. Although group drama is practised a great deal, there seems to be a move in some circles away from small group work to whole class work. One of the objections is that unless children 'show' their work it is extremely difficult to gauge what progress they are making.

The problems of evaluation

The question of whether it is possible to assess or evaluate progress is one of the main issues being discussed at present. One reason for this is that non-specialists are asking whether teachers can prove that drama has taught children anything. Also the subject has progressed further from the point where drama teachers vaguely felt that teaching the subject must be good, to their wanting to be more explicit about what they are achieving.

Not all drama teachers feel that it is necessary to evaluate work. Some teachers feel that any attempt to evaluate might detract from spontaneity – which is so vital in all creative activities. Others feel that the end products of drama, like any other art form, are open ended and unpredictable. They feel that because of this there are no clearly defined criteria that could be used in assessing drama. There is a feeling that it is not possible to evaluate work in terms of aims, objectives and end products and therefore attempts to assess drama might distort an appreciation of the complexity of the process.

These arguments point out the problems involved in assessment. However, if teachers make claims for certain kinds of development in drama, it seems reasonable to expect them to back their claims up by examples of success or failure. As yet there is no clearly defined body of knowledge concerning the evaluation of development in drama. A number of academic dissertations have been written on the subject. In recent conferences on drama teaching numerous attempts have been made to link drama with current theories on child development, especially with play and theories about the artistic process.

One of the areas in which serious attempts have been made to evaluate what happens in drama lessons is in that of forming criteria in which to examine drama. More teachers are taking Advanced Drama Board examinations which concentrate on examining educational drama. With the increasing trend of examinations in C.S.E. and G.C.E. in upper schools, more ways of examining children are being devised. As yet no satisfactory overall means of examination seem to have been found. In examining teachers, such questions as 'How do you think the lesson went?' or 'How would you develop the work now?' are asked. In these cases it is extremely easy for the examiner to rely on subjective notions of whether he thought the teacher's work worthwhile or not.

I have seen children assessed for C.S.E. examinations on vastly differing criteria, ranging from marks on effort and enthusiasm to strictly marked scales for theatrical skills, e.g. five ways of using the voice differently. Between these extremes are general criteria such as 'ability to characterise' or 'general ability to use communication skills on stage and in real life'.

It seems that there is a great deal more work to be done before the overall standards of examining can be maintained and that there is a need for tighter criteria for what is being examined so that subjective decisions about work can be minimised. These criteria would need to be formed in such a way that maximum flexibility was allowed to enable the creative process to flourish. For instance, in small group improvisations, it could be argued that what is being judged is the children's personal statement of ideas in dramatic form, and, if they perform it, whether they are putting the statement across effectively. The problem here is how to sieve out an observer's subjective interpretation of the children's work, leaving only an objective assessment about the quality of the work. It is the same problem that theatre critics have about plays and performances. The question is whether it should be examined, i.e. given marks or not.

Examinations

It is not just the problem of evaluating that makes the topic of examinations such a crucial one. More and more pupils are being offered drama as an examination subject, sometimes because teachers genuinely believe that children work better under the pressure of a well thought out course which has an examination as a focal point.

However, not all teachers agree with examinations. Some feel that the drama they teach encourages group cooperation and that it would be counter-productive to introduce an element of competition. There is an argument that in drama the process is more important than the end product and that the creative process involves learning for enjoyment and for its own sake. For these teachers, the main aims and central concepts of drama teaching run counter to the subject based, individualistic, competitive notions of education in examination oriented schools. The main advantage of drama is that it offers the children a way of working without the pressure of examinations – an alternative way.

These arguments again reflect the fact that there are a number of reasons why drama is taught. It seems to me that the question of examinations becomes important only if there is increasing pressure on teachers to base their work on preparing for examinations. This could prove extremely restricting to those teachers who do not place importance on the achievement of end products in drama.

In returning to the question of evaluation, it seems that at present there is uncertainty about what is being assessed and how certain activities can be evaluated in practical terms. This is because in drama there seem to be few clearly defined criteria for evaluation and teachers have not studied what happens in the classroom in enough detail to be able to spot development when it occurs. This is not to say that they do not have criteria or do not make judgements about work in the classroom. They do, but often on unconscious, implicit levels which they find difficult to define. A theoretical framework could provide a starting point for teachers who wish to evaluate their work.

The need for a theoretical framework for drama teaching

At present there is no general overview of the variety of practices found in drama teaching. Neither has a theoretical basis been given for the distinctive nature of the subject and its specific contributions to children's development. A theoretical framework is therefore needed which gives a coherent theoretical structure characterising and reflecting the variety of practices possible in drama teaching.

The need for such a framework has been recognised by the Schools Council which has funded a project on drama teaching to 'Clarify aims and objectives of drama teaching, and to find ways of evaluating outcomes where possible'. The project is looking in depth at the work of a number of teachers in six areas in England. An attempt is being made to establish a theoretical base for these teachers' work and to see how each teacher's work develops over a year.

1 Attempts are being made to provide a rationale for drama teaching by looking at those activities and aims which could be said to be common to all drama teaching. The question 'What is there about drama teaching that defines it as "drama teaching"' is being asked. Once the distinctive nature of the subject is clearly defined, it is then possible to see whether the activity itself could develop children in certain ways, regardless of what drama method is being used.

For instance, some generalisations might be made concerning the ability of children to react within a 'drama' situation – whether the activities are based on mime, are teacher directed or child centred. In all situations they have to act within a dramatic structure demanding 'pretence' and inventiveness on the one hand, and accurate perception on the other hand, if the work is to be convincing. For example, if the boys in the mime case described were not able to create the illusions of elephants and flies accurately enough to be understood by an audience, their point about lethal doses coming in all sizes would have been meaningless.

Although I have tried to look at some of the common elements in the five case studies described, a more detailed and sophisticated examination of the issues and practices involved is required. Notions of, for example, imagination, creativity and 'acting' need to be taken further not only in terms of their possible educational functions, but also in terms of the kinds of developments that could occur within 'dramatic activities' found in all drama lessons.

2 The variety of approaches and activities are being examined in detail. Each approach should be studied with a view to defining what it contains and what its implications are for the types of development teachers wish to work towards. Because teachers in drama can use more than one method for getting effects, the different activities available to them in drama ought to be seen in the light of the kinds of development they might or might not achieve.

The future place of drama in schools

THE PROBLEMS OF TIMETABLING

Drama will not be generally accepted as a legitimate educational activity unless the subject is backed by theory and seen to work. However, even when it is accepted educational administrators will need to know how various forms of drama could fit into timetables. How the subject is timetabled would depend on the kind of drama schools want to have and what a particular teacher's emphases are. For instance, if drama is to be used as a service subject it will probably only occur when there is a special need for it within a subject. It would be impossible to timetable it as such although in cases of this kind there are times when teachers may have the use of the hall or a space.

On the other hand, if the subject is given a status in its own right, more continuous time will be needed if children are to be encouraged to develop it as far as they can. Children doing group improvisations need time to establish constructive working relationships, to experiment as much as they need in order to be able to work on and shape their ideas. They also require time to establish their own criteria of excellence and to work until they are satisfied with what they are doing. There will be periods when a particular group will become interested in exploring a particular issue in their own terms, e.g. the question of Women's Liberation, and will want to work on that until they have come to terms with it. All this requires some form of continuity and would not be possible if children were given one-off lessons of thirty minutes a week; in very short lessons, children are usually just getting down to work by the time the bell rings. Before drama is timetabled in any school, it is important for a drama teacher to have a clear idea of what he wants. More thought therefore needs to be given to how much time various approaches to drama might require so that drama teachers have a firm practical basis from which to argue. Research needs to be done not only on the nature of the development of various activities, but also on kinds of timetables that have been put into practice with reference to their advantages and disadvantages. It may also be that different age groups require different periods of time. As far as I know no detailed research has yet been conducted along these lines although evidence concerning the needs of children of different age groups would be helpful in negotiating for space and time in schools.

How any subject is timetabled depends on a number of criteria; for instance, what its status is as regards other subjects. Drama does not enjoy a high status compared to many other subjects. Convincing argument might go some way towards increasing the amount of drama in schools, but does not necessarily mean that the subject should or would be given priority over other subjects. Very often schools are timetabled according to a particular pattern and subjects have to fit into this pattern. It might be useful to look at some of the ways in which drama is currently timetabled and at what future trends might be.

It seems that the most predominant pattern in the first two years is a single or double period for drama once a week. This gives pupils time to acquire some skills such as movement and to do some drama. Many children at this stage, however, incorporate an element of play (i.e. unstructured work – make believe for the sake of it) before beginning to shape their work. They sometimes complain that they do not have enough time to see their work through. It is, however, questionable whether if they were given more time they would produce better work.

Two other forms of timetabling are emerging, especially in comprehensive schools. These are block timetabling and the modular system. With block timetabling, subjects are divided into faculties and each faculty is given a block of time. It is then up to the members of a faculty how they use their time. A 'creative arts' faculty can, for instance, consist of art, music, drama and dance. Time is divided so that children can experience some time with each subject. A common way to divide the time is for each subject to be given a block of time for three weeks. For instance, children might spend three hours at a stretch doing drama for three weeks and then switch over to another subject. The advantage of this is that there is enough time to accomplish something of quality at one stretch. This can often give pupils the satisfying feeling that they have achieved something that is more or less finished. By having a lot of time concentrated over a short period, children can remember what went immediately before and build from that. This method is satisfactory with experienced teachers who have enough resources to work profitably for three hours, but not many teachers are trained to work in this way, with the result that they find it difficult to fill in the time and children get bored. Another problem with this kind of timetabling is that the children might forget much of what they have done by the time they return to a subject after a term or so, with the result that the teacher may have to start from the beginning if the pupils are to achieve the same amount of concentration that they had at the end of their last three week period.

In a modular timetable, where time is divided into fifteen minute modules, there is more flexibility for teachers to negotiate for the amount of time they think pupils should have at a particular stage of their work. For instance, a teacher might want to do a series of lessons on constructing village life which may require a lot of time, but as soon as the series is completed another teacher could take over. However, relations between staff need to be good for each teacher to get his fair share.

In some 'creative arts' faculties the teachers may combine resources to treat a certain theme – e.g. 'ritual'. For example, the art teacher helps make masks, the dance teacher organises ritual dances, the music teacher contributes instruments and music and the drama teacher shapes it all together into a dramatic sequence, using acting and speech as well as music and dance. If it works well, this kind of teaching can work to the advantage of the drama teacher because he can enrich his own work by using additional media.

Most drama is still taught in the English department. Here, drama can be used as a natural extension of English or vice versa. The problem with drama within an English department is that it is either not seen as a subject in its own right, or it is taught as if it had nothing to do with English and therefore loses its relevance. If drama is timetabled within the English department, it usually means that it is largely taught by non-specialists, often teachers who do not know much about the subject. In these cases the drama specialist is often used to advise and help other teachers. It might be argued, however, that if children are to develop within drama and to use the medium to its fullest advantage, specialist training is necessary.

Drama departments can be useful because they give the subject individual status, and they ensure the presence of more than one specialist in the school. This usually means that the subject is available to more pupils although often it is the non-academic children, e.g. remedial classes, who receive the extra drama teaching. One of the major disadvantages of drama departments is that drama teachers often find themselves teaching in isolation. In cases where the subject is not fully respected this can place the teachers in a difficult position.

There is an increasing trend for drama teachers to offer drama as an examination subject in the upper school. This means that work tends to become more formalised the older the children get. This may or may not be a good idea depending what the teacher's approach to the subject is. For example, if the teacher feels that the acquisition of performance skills trains pupils for performance and that this can be examined, it would be legitimate to have examinations. If, on the other hand, a teacher uses whole class playmaking to encourage decisionmaking and the understanding of various topics, he may think examinations an inappropriate way of testing success. Yet even in cases of this sort, teachers often offer examinations: the advantage for children of having a piece of paper at the end of a course is an important aspect to take into account.

PUBLIC PERFORMANCES

So far I have looked at the way in which drama is organised in the timetable. There is another factor that needs to be taken into account when discussing the role of the drama teacher within the school. That is the pressure put upon the specialist to direct public performances for the school. Most drama teachers enjoy this and many schools allow them some time off during school time for rehearsals near the date of the performance. Productions can, however, create a number of difficulties. Rehearsals often have to take place outside school times. This means that the drama teacher is doing a lot of additional work outside his normal teaching time. Rehearsing can be physically and emotionally exhausting, demands can be made on the teacher at all times during the school day. Spare time needs to be found to organise buying of props, costumes etc. Fatigue can often affect his classroom work in which case the children's work suffers. In some schools teachers have to leave their classes alone in order to rehearse. This does not aid the continuous development of the subject and ought to be considered when pressures are put on drama teachers to organise activities outside their ordinary teaching load.

In the last few pages I have mentioned a few of the ways in which drama can be organised in schools and have discussed the main pressure which drama teachers sometimes have outside their normal loads. I have by no means exhausted the range of possibilities. For instance, it might be possible to have a concentrated course of drama once a year after which there would be examinations where children could work, e.g., towards performances or towards exploring a theme. Drama specialists could have part of their timetable as floating teachers so that other subject teachers could incorporate drama as a service subject and have a specialist to teach it for them.

To return to the point made at the beginning of this chapter, people need to be clear about the kinds of drama required in the school and the special interests and demands that drama teachers in each school make. There is a need for teachers to be aware of the demands on time and facilities that their particular approaches may make. Studies should be made of existing ways in which drama is being taught in schools so that all the possibilities and problems are known in advance.

The organisation of drama on the timetable is important. As important is a consideration of the facilities available to teachers teaching the subject.

SPACE FOR DRAMA TEACHING

Many schools do not have special facilities for drama teaching. In the case studies mentioned, only one school had a specially built drama studio. Two other schools had drama rooms, neither of which were adequate: one was too small; the other was used for a number of purposes, including classroom work and school lunches, which meant that equipment could never be left out and that the room was full of furniture. In one school, drama was taught in a gymnasium where there was too much space and in which sound echoed. Drama is often conducted in year rooms or school halls, in both of which lessons are constantly interrupted by people passing through or getting ready for dinners. Teachers using public spaces such as halls are continually required to find other places to work because the space is required for examinations or for special occasions. The inadequate conditions in which drama teachers have to work often reflects the fact that the subject is not taken seriously. Often, even if headmasters are willing to provide space for drama, old school buildings have not been planned to incorporate such subjects. There is frequently a genuine lack of space which affects the whole school. This is especially the case in primary schools.

Lack of adequate facilities can often prevent drama teachers from achieving as much as they would like. This is because space and an environment in which children feel they can work unhindered is a prerequisite for drama teaching. One of the ways in which children express themselves in drama is physically. To do this they need to be able to experiment with movement and space. They must have room to move. If they are working in small groups they need space to get away from each other. If they are working as a class, they need space to move from one place to another. They cannot do this in small spaces or in rooms which are full of desks. The use of speech is important in most dramatic activities. Often people need to raise their voices in order to get the dramatic effect they want. If children are placed in rooms where they have to be careful to be quiet, work either becomes inhibited or they are constantly interrupted with requests to keep quiet. A space is therefore required in which children can use their voices without feeling restricted.

There are times when children wish to create physical environments in which to work, e.g. constructions with chairs symbolising caves. If the activity occurs over a period of time, it is useful to have the constructions available for use without having to reconstruct them and take them down every time. Often there is little space to store props or sets made for performances. A space in which there is room to store things and perhaps set things up for the next lesson would be extremely useful for most drama teachers. It also enables them to create physical environments if they wish to set up working atmospheres different from that of a plain classroom, for example, that of a mock television studio.

Sound and lighting equipment can be useful in creating atmosphere in drama lessons. Most teachers have access either to tape recorders or record players. Fewer have access to lighting as a normal teaching prop unless they are using the school stage for theatre training. However, where new schools have been built or are being designed, drama studios are being equipped with sound and lighting equipment that can usually be used by the children as part of their work as well as by the teacher. In some schools video equipment is also being installed so that children can look at their work or, if they wish, produce their own programmes on video.

It is difficult to ascertain trends in designs for drama studios. At one time it was popular to paint the walls black. Some teachers blocked out windows because they felt that children would be less distracted. This phase has passed and I have seen the other extreme where a gallery has been built around the studio so that visitors can come in at any time to observe what is going on. Most teachers would be content simply with a space of their own in which a creative working atmosphere can be created so that children come in, enjoy themselves and work hard to achieve a reasonable standard of work.

As can be seen, the question of facilities for drama is vital if good work is to be produced. This is not to say that worthwhile drama has not occurred in cloakrooms, crowded classrooms or echoing halls. It has been taught in difficult conditions through the efforts of good teachers. How much better the work could be, then, if working conditions were improved.

Because of the importance of space in the teaching of drama, this should be a major consideration when staff are thinking of incorporating drama in the timetable. Teaching drama without proper space is a little like trying to teach pupils chemistry without any chemicals.

Summary

In this chapter I have attempted to give some indication of present trends in drama. In theoretical thinking there is a move away from areas of controversy such as 'theatre' versus 'creative drama' towards the need for a conceptual framework for drama teaching. This conceptual framework should not only indicate what the distinctive nature of drama teaching is but also state clearly what contributions drama teaching can make to education in general. In addition, the framework should allow for the flexible nature of drama teaching in which a number of different approaches and different methods of teaching are possible.

There is a move in some circles to try to evaluate drama work. It was argued that this could not be done without a firm theoretical basis to start with and that a great deal of work would need to be done before reasonable attempts at evaluation could be possible.

Trends towards attempts to define more clearly what drama teaching is about and how work can be assessed stem from a number of current developments in drama. Drama teachers themselves are at a stage when they wish to articulate their ideas more fully and to discover ways in which they can assess their own work and the development of their pupils. Conflicting external pressures mean that there is a demand for drama specialists to produce a well thought out rationale for the subject and some proof that drama teaching has a special contribution to make. On the one hand, more people are interested in and want to try the subject. They need clear guidelines as to what the subject claims to do, the sorts of criteria used for standards of work, and ideas on the range of activities possible. On the other hand, the current financial situation means that drama, along with other subjects, is having to fight for its existence and is having to make clear and explicit cases for why drama budgets should not be cut.

This may be one of the reasons why there is an increasing trend towards drama as an examination subject in the fourth and fifth years in secondary schools. Examinations in drama have their advantages and disadvantages and teachers are having to think carefully about their priorities before they commit themselves.

Because of increased interest in the subject itself, teachers are being asked to give policy decisions about the amount of time needed for drama to be taught effectively. There is increasing need for teachers and administrators to be aware of the various ways in which drama can be organised in schools. They should also have some ideas on how different kinds of organisation could affect the development of drama in a particular school and whether organising drama in a certain way would best suit the kind of drama being offered by the teachers in that school.

People are becoming more aware of the problems produced by pressures on the drama teacher to produce public performances over and above their normal work loads. A number of teachers are refusing to put on school performances and an increasing number of headteachers are making allowances for performances when planning the teacher's timetable. This, however, is not generally thought about and needs to be considered by headteachers if they want drama in their schools to function efficiently.

Another factor influencing the nature and quality of drama work is space. Space and a working environment is essential if drama is to be taught effectively. It is no use having a theoretical basis which justifies drama teaching when the development of the subject in a school cannot be given a fair chance because of inadequate conditions.

11 Summary and conclusion

The first part of this book dealt with the present state of drama. The kinds of drama that can be found in schools were described. Some of the justifications for the teaching of the subject were discussed. It was argued that the activity of drama helps to encourage greater understanding of people and their situations, both on wider social and interpersonal levels. Drama is a valuable form of communication and because expression in drama is verbal and physical, it gives people the opportunity to express themselves more effectively in everyday situations. Drama is a social activity. It encourages children to work creatively together and to work on and solve problems of interest to them. It gives groups the opportunity to make dramatic statements about the way they see and interpret people and situations. As well as the value of the activities of drama for children's development, it has value on a wider cultural level. 'Drama' or 'theatre' is a recognised art form. The finished art forms (plays, reviews, etc.) have been used throughout the ages to communicate particular interpretations of people and their feelings and thoughts to the community. Drama is a part of people's everyday lives, experienced through the mass media as well as in the traditional theatre. The emergence of community theatre groups and theatre in education teams indicates that there is an increasing awareness of the importance of this form of communication. If the teaching of other arts such as the visual arts and music is considered relevant in schools today, it would be odd if drama were left out of the curriculum. However, although there is some support for drama teaching in schools, the subject is not yet fully recognised. Figures published in the Bullock Report support this view.

Lack of full recognition may be due to continuing uncertainty about the theoretical basis behind drama teaching. An attempt was made to outline some of the central concepts and activities found in written work about drama teaching. These include concepts such as imagination and creativity, play and social development.

One of the problems of establishing a rationale for drama teaching is that there are a number of controversial issues in drama about which there is little agreement; for instance, whether children should show their work or not, or whether there is any place for discussions in drama lessons. I have suggested that examples of bad practice are often used as excuses for dismissing perfectly legitimate approaches to drama. This is because people fail to take the flexible nature of drama into account and to allow for the fact that there are a number of possibilities open to those who wish to teach drama.

Examples of five possible ways of teaching drama were given in an attempt to show that questions raised about controversial issues should be seen in the context of particular approaches and methods. For instance, discussion is perfectly relevant for the teacher who wishes children to consider the general effects of miners' strikes, but not so relevant for the teacher who wants his children to work on their own at their own levels. Examples of the use of movement and formal mime; teacher directed class drama; child centred group improvisation; drama as a service subject and as a theatre art were given. In cases where lessons were part of sequences, the whole sequence was mentioned so that the work could be seen in context.

Although examples of work give an idea of the practical aspects of drama, it is important to look at current thinking on the subject if the development of drama is to be discussed. Present trends in drama teaching concern the question of evaluation and the problems of examinations in drama. It was suggested that there was a move away from the polarisation of theoretical positions towards the formulation of a theoretical framework that would encompass the wide range of approaches and practices possible in drama. There is a growing awareness that if the subject is to develop as fully as possible, certain demands need to be made on schools with regard to staffing, timetabling and facilities. It is important that teachers are sure of their objectives and are able to explain to headteachers and the wider public, including parents, what the requirements of their particular kind of drama might be.

Finally, it seems that the main area needing more thought and research is in the study of the actual processes involved in different ways of teaching drama. In-depth studies need to be made over a period of time to ascertain what kinds of learning are involved and the possible developmental sequences children may undergo when being taught drama. This kind of research could be invaluable to those concerned with evaluation.

One major theme of this book has been that there are various ways in which drama can be taught, all for different purposes. More work needs to be done on the different educational functions drama can have within the school curriculum and the ways in which drama can be integrated into the organisational structures of various schools.

Not only is there a need for drama specialists to clarify their own aims and objectives and to think more about what is happening in the classroom, but there is also a need for non-specialists to see drama in a general educational context. Until there is more general recognition of the value of the subject possibilities for its rapid development are limited.

References *and* Name index

ALLEN, J. (1967) Drama. *Education Survey* 2. London, H.M.S.O. *10*

BOLTON, G. (1971) Drama and theatre in education: a survey. In Dodd (1971). *15*

BULLOCK REPORT (1975) Oral language. Chapter 10 of *A Language for Life*. London, H.M.S.O. *107*

DODD, N. (1971) (ed.) *Drama and Theatre in Education*. London, Faber and Faber. *11, 12, 15*

HEATHCOTE, D. (1971) Drama and education: subject or method? In Dodd (1971). *11, 12, 16*

HODGSON, J. and RICHARDS, E. (1966) *Improvisation*. London, Methuen. *12, 13*

MCGREGOR, L. (1975) A sociological investigation of drama teaching in three schools, pp. 137–214. Unpublished M.Phil thesis, Institute of Education, London. *4–41, 42–60*

ROBINSON, K. (1975) Find a space. Mimeo, University of London Schools Examinations Department. *5–7*

SLADE, P. (1954) *Child Drama*. Cambridge, Cambridge University Press. *11, 14*

SLADE, P. (1958) Drama therapy as an aid to becoming a person. *Guild of Pastoral Psychology*, **June 1958**. *11, 14*

SLADE, P. (1964) *Introduction to Child Drama*. Cambridge, Cambridge University Press. *11, 14*

SLADE, P. (1968) *Experience in Spontaneity*. Harlow, Longmans. *11, 14*

WAY, B. (1969) *Development Through Drama*. Harlow, Longmans. *12, 14, 15*

Subject index